BETTER TO LIGHT

ONE CANDLE

Better to Light One Candle

THE CHRISTOPHERS'

Three Minutes a Day

MILLENNIAL EDITION

A GINIGER BOOK
PUBLISHED IN ASSOCIATION WITH
CONTINUUM NEW YORK

1999

The Continuum Publishing Company
370 Lexington Avenue, New York, NY 10017

Published in association with the K.S. Giniger Company, Inc.
250 West 57th Street, New York, NY 10017

Copyright 2000 by The Christophers

Printed in the United States of America

Better to light one candle : the Christophers' Three minutes a day.
    --Millennial ed.
         p.   cm.
      ISBN 0-8264-1163-0
      1. Meditations.   2. Devotional calendars.
   I. Christophers (Organization)
   BV4812.A1B48   1999
   242' .2--dc21

Scripture quotations in this publication are from the Revised Standard Version Bible, Catholic Edition, copyright 1965 and 1966 by the Division of Christian Education of the National Council of Churches of Christ in the U.S.A. and the New Revised Standard Version Bible, Catholic Edition, copyright 1989 by the Division of Christian Education of the National Council of Churches of Christ in the United States of America and used by permission.

The Christophers

REV. THOMAS J. MCSWEENEY
Director

STEPHANIE RAHA
Editor-in-chief

MARGARET O'CONNELL
Senior Research Editor

ALISON MORAN
MARY RIDDLE
JOSEPII THOMAS
Contributing Editors

UMBERTO MIGNARDI
ANNA MARIE TRIPODI
Editorial Services

12 EAST 48TH STREET
NEW YORK, NY 10017
TEL: 212-759-4050
WWW.CHRISTOPHERS.ORG

In the beginning was the Word,
and the Word was with God,
and the Word was God.
He was in the beginning with God.
All things came into being through Him,
and without Him not one thing came into being.
What has come into being in Him was life,
and the life was the light of all people.
The light shines in the darkness,
and the darkness did not overcome it.

John 1:1-5

Introduction

It's better to light one candle than to curse the darkness.

When Father James Keller, M.M., founded The Christophers in 1945, he chose that ancient Chinese proverb as the motto, the credo for the movement. He was convinced that each person is uniquely important, that everyone has a personal responsibility to change the world for the better, and that positive action can work miracles.

From our beginnings, The Christophers have used the print and electronic media to remind people of their God-given mission to serve our loving Creator by serving our brothers and sisters.

From *Christopher News Notes* in English and Spanish to *Light One Candle* newspaper columns, from radio spots and the weekly *Christopher Closeup* television series to annual Christopher Awards and our Internet Web site (www. christophers.org), we still share our message of hope.

Father Keller wrote the first *Three Minutes a Day* book of daily reflections in 1949, believing "that the most effective exterior action had to come from a strong interior spirituality."

"For one reason or another, most people don't devote much time to developing this quality. They tend to get entangled in the cares and burdens of daily existence and forget the big meaning of life. If some sort of pattern could be devised that would encourage individuals to set aside even a few minutes a day to pray and meditate on such questions as "Why am I here? Where did I come from? Where am I going?" it could give countless individuals a perspective of eternity."

He felt that individuals with this outlook would want to do more than just get through each day; they would want to make it count for something. *Three Minutes a Day* would be the spiritual note, the motivation, that he wanted to inject into the lives of everyone who could be reached through the Christopher movement.

The popular book series has continued thanks to the contributions of many men and women over the years. With a story or anecdote for each day of the year plus a scripture verse and a prayer, every volume offers inspiration for each day of the year.

We are delighted to issue this special thirty-fourth volume, our Millennial Edition, with The Continuum Publishing Company. It is a collection of some of our best stories from several volumes. And, to make it a true perennial, we have added a separate section for movable feasts and holidays.

Today, on the brink of a new millenium, many people are showing a renewed interest in spiritual matters as well as in the future of our world. We hope that this book will encourage them – and you – on this journey.

And may you light many candles – for yourself, for loved ones and neighbors, for generations to come.

Father Tom McSweeney
Director of The Christophers

Positive Beginnings

There are lots of superstitions about New Year's Day. Many of them involve foods that are supposed to bring good luck for the coming year.

For instance, Pennsylvanians have a tradition of eating pork and avoiding turkey on New Year's Day. The reason is, a turkey scratches backward, but a pig roots forward representing a forward-looking approach to the new year.

Even if superstitions about food have no real basis, the value of a forward-looking approach is unquestionable.

Instead of dwelling on past mistakes or bad luck, we need to make constructive plans for the future. A positive outlook coupled with determination are more important than "luck" in shaping our lives.

New Year's Day may be associated with making resolutions, but any day is a good time for a fresh start if we choose to make it so.

You have been born anew, not of perishable but of imperishable seed, through the living and enduring word of God. (1 Peter 1:23)

Renew us each day, Holy Spirit.

A Most Human Prayer

The Jewish Theological Seminary of America took a full page ad in the *New York Times* a while back to say Happy New Year to people of all faiths or no faith.

It contained some memorable words on prayer: "Start small. Bless one moment for what it brings you. Say one ancient prayer, link yourself with continuity and eternity. Fill one silence with your end of the conversation. No one can do this for you; it belongs to you."

Jew, Christian, Muslim, other faiths – is there a believer who could not profit from these suggestions? A non-believer who could not find food for thought?

Only we humans can believe, can pray, can speak – with words or with silence. Start a conversation with God. Enter His peaceful presence.

Prayer is a truly human activity that links us with the Divine. It's the perfect way to begin the year.

[Jesus] would withdraw to deserted places and pray. (Luke 5:16)

Lord, teach me to welcome You, to listen to You, to speak with You each day.

On This Island Earth

Some three and a half centuries ago, when John Donne wrote, "No man is an island," an island seemed totally isolated, untouched by the rest of the world.

A few years ago, a scientist visited a deserted island in the Pacific. It was about 300 miles from the nearest inhabited island and 3,000 miles from a continent. But he found bottles and plastic debris scattered on the beach.

Today, even more than in Donne's time, our lives affect the lives of many others. Irresponsible behavior in one part of the world – whether in the form of pollution or warfare – now threatens the welfare of people everywhere.

You are a citizen of the larger community: "a piece of the continent, a part of the main." And distant shores are not so distant any more.

There are varieties of gifts . . . varieties of services . . . varieties of activities, but it is the same God who activates all of them in everyone.
(I Corinthians 12:4–6)

Thank You for my unique talents; and for the opportunity to use them for good, Creator.

Seeing All Life's Colors

Some people literally see the world in a rosier light than others.

Apples and rubies and fire engines look redder to them. And their eyes can distinguish slight variations in the shades of red between, say, two red shirts that look identical to other people.

Recent studies show that a difference in just one amino acid makes this difference in color vision. It affects the way certain specialized cells of the eye absorb red light.

How you see color is determined by heredity. It's beyond your control.

But how you see life is up to you. You can choose to live joyfully no matter what your circumstances — by trusting in God's love. Your attitude is always up to you.

Thus says the Lord. . . "Do not fear, for I have redeemed you; I have called you by name, you are Mine. . . . you are precious in My sight, and honored, and I love you." (Isaiah 43:1, 4)

Creator and Redeemer, You do love me and protect me. Enable me to appreciate Your love!

Words of Wisdom from "Silent Cal"

President Calvin Coolidge was called "Silent Cal," because he was a taciturn individual. But though he used words sparingly did not mean that he lacked wisdom or the ability to articulate a sound idea.

Once, for instance, he had this to say: "People criticize me for harping on the obvious. Perhaps someday I'll write an article on "The Importance of the Obvious."

"If all the folks in the United States would do the few simple things they know they ought to do, most of our big problems would take care of themselves."

There is a tendency to write such remarks off as simplistic. Attention to duty alone isn't going to solve the problems of homelessness, poverty, illiteracy and the like. At the same time, however, these are all situations which can yield to citizen action, whether the action be taken individually or in concert with others.

To the extent that an individual contributes to the overall good, then he or she is doing something to make things better than they had been.

Whoever is faithful in a very little is faithful also in much; and whoever is dishonest in a very little is dishonest also in much. (Luke 16:10)

Lord, help me use the talents You have given me to make things a little bit better for all.

Just for Today

I'd like to share some "just for today" suggestions for you to take along to work with you. Just for today . . .

- be friendly and pleasant with co-workers
- try to see the good in every situation
- do all your work to the best of your ability
- find something to praise in every person
- be happy you're alive, well, and employed
- do not compare yourself with anyone else
- leave work looking forward to the evening, thankful for what you've accomplished

Just for today . . . and tomorrow . . . and the next day. Soon your workplace will be a better place for your being part of it. And, after all, isn't that one thing we all want to accomplish — just for today?

Jesus of Nazareth . . . went about doing good. (Acts 10:38)

Inspired by Your example, Jesus, may I also do good.

His Home Was a Box

Alexander Wortley, an Englishman, chose to live in a small box until his death at age eighty. His box measured three feet wide, four feet long, and five feet high. It had wheels, was made of wood except for a metal roof, and was painted green. Furnishings consisted of an old bus seat and shelves to hold food and belongings.

Wortley pulled his mini-trailer all over England, stopping wherever he wanted to but never living anyplace except in his box. In the last twenty years of his life, he worked as the caretaker of a secluded cottage in Buckinghamshire. But his job had no effect at all on his lifestyle. He parked his box at one side of the garden and continued to live in it.

Few of us would voluntarily live in such cramped quarters. Yet psychologically we may be confining ourselves in a box that we have built.

For instance, if we think we have no special ability, we never try to do creative things. And if we will never use our talent, we will never believe we have it.

We can step out of the box of our own making and stand tall if we realize that we do have a special gift from God. And using it will make this world a better place.

Every perfect gift is from above, coming down from the Father of lights. (James 1:17)

Creator, help me discover the special talent You have given me.

A Great Singer

Opera singer Luigi Lablache is considered one of the greatest basses of the mid-nineteenth century. But opera then offered few leading roles for a bass, so between leads, he sang minor parts.

A colleague once remarked that Lablache was wasted in the small part he was singing at the time. Lablache replied, "My friend, to a great singer there are no small parts. And to a small singer there are no great ones."

Sometimes we may feel that our role in life is only a small one. But every role is important when it's done well. Instead of dwelling on limits, we need to focus on excellence.

To each is given the manifestation of the Spirit for the common good. (1 Corinthians 12:7)

Giver of every good gift, inspire us to use our gifts for the common good.

Homeless, Not Friendless

For forty years, John Nelson walked the streets of Brooklyn, one of the army of homeless people who wander in and around every city of any size the world over.

But John Nelson had dignity and his friends, the people of the neighborhood, helped him retain it.

Dr. Wayne Longmore and his family regularly shared their Sunday dinner with him. Charlotte Atkins, a florist, helped him obtain Social Security. She and her husband invited Nelson to sleep in their store. Neighbors stopped to talk with him.

When John Nelson died of a heart attack, one neighbor organized a memorial service. Fifty people attended and they planted a flowering shrub over his grave.

Speaking at that service, Dr. Longmore said, "We were John's family." "There was something about him that was blessed and special," said Lisa Feldman. Another friend said, "You take care of your own, and he was our own. . . . He had a different kind of dignity."

God gave each person dignity when He made us. Sometimes circumstances make it hard to recognize our own dignity or to see it in others. But it is always there, if we see through God's eyes.

How does God's love abide in anyone who has the world's goods and sees a brother or sister in need yet refuses to help? (1 John 3:17)

Merciful Savior, help me to imitate Your compassion.

Presidential Hospitality

Grace Tully worked as a personal secretary for Franklin and Eleanor Roosevelt for more than thirty years.

Right up to the time of her death, she spoke with admiration about the way they treated her. With the Roosevelts, she said, you were never considered just the help. You were considered part of the family.

She recalls that if you were working late and Eleanor Roosevelt was aware of it, she would order another chair be put at the dinner table so you could eat with the family. That special touch of hospitality made all the difference.

Real hospitality goes beyond mere politeness to guests. It is a commitment to the golden rule. It includes one's fellows and strangers as well. Be hospitable. Do to others as you would have them do to you.

You shall love the Lord your God with all your heart, and with all your soul, and with all your strength, and with all your mind. (Luke 10:27)

How can my love for You, Jesus, grow truer? How can I welcome You today?

The Work of His Hands

Here's some good advice from a second century bishop, Irenaeus of Lyon, about our relationship with our Creator.

> You are the work of God,
> await the hand of the Artist
> who does all things in due season.
> Offer Him your heart, soft and
> tractable and keep the form in
> which the Artist has fashioned you.
> Let the clay (of your being) be moist,
> lest you grow hard
> And lose the imprint of His fingers.

Centuries before Irenacus, the prophet Jeremiah wrote that we are like clay in the potter's hand – God's hand.

We need only be willing to be shaped by our Maker to His plans for us.

"Can I not do with you . . . as this potter has done?" says the Lord. "Just like the clay in the potter's hand, so are you in My hand." (Jeremiah 18:6)

Master Potter, form me, fashion me, into a fit vessel for Your Spirit.

Shapers of Our World

Richard and Rhoda Goldman established the Goldman Environmental Prizes to encourage grass roots support of the environment. Among prize winners from around the world were:

Chinese journalist Dai Qing who criticized a proposed dam on the Yangtze River.

Joann Tall, a Lakota, who fought nuclear weapons testing and toxic waste dumping on Native American lands.

Margaret Jacobson and her husband, Garth Owen-Sith, who organized a community-based solution to wild-life poaching in Namibia.

Most of us will not win awards for our efforts. But the least thing we do to support our environment brings its own reward — a more livable, humane world. And that should be prize enough.

Do not invite death by the error of your life, or bring on destruction by the works of your hands; because God did not make death, and He does not delight in the death of the living.
(Wisdom of Solomon 1:12-13)

May all our deeds be life-giving, Creator.

Promoting Peace

A group of New England writers once held an unusual peace demonstration in Massachusetts.

They invited the public to come and listen as they read prose and poetry proclaiming that life is precious and war is terrible.

The program was organized to give writers a way of demonstrating their concern for peace. Their point was that peace is the work of everyone — including those who aren't certain where to start.

One way all of us can make peace a reality in our own lives is through prayer. Another is to associate with other people who are concerned about peace. Read about it. Talk about it. Live it.

Be a peacemaker to the world — starting within your own heart.

If it is possible, so far as it depends on you, live peaceably with all. (Romans 12:18)

Lord, help me accept Your peace into my own heart.

Chasing Happiness

It seems a big dog was watching a smaller dog chase its tail. "What are you doing?" he asked.

"I'm looking for happiness," the small dog said. "Someone told me that happiness is in my tail and when I catch it I will be happy."

The big dog replied that he had heard that, too. But he discovered that every time he chased his tail it ran away from him. "So, now," he said, "I just relax and do what dogs are supposed to do and I find that happiness comes to me."

If you're running around in circles trying to find happiness, why not just relax and do what humans are supposed to do. Love God and your neighbor and yourself. And, perhaps, not so surprisingly, happiness will find you.

May [Christ] dwell in your hearts through faith, as you are being rooted and grounded in love. (Ephesians 3:17)

Abide within me, Jesus.

Sing Out Loud

If there is one activity that most people seem to enjoy, it's singing. We sing in the car, the shower, or when we're home alone.

When we sing, we relax and enjoy ourselves. Experts have found that singing is good for you. It elevates the spirit, it helps to express thoughts and feelings, and it provides an emotional release. Humans are the only animal with a fully developed voice that can be used for speaking and singing.

And from choirs to old-fashioned sing-alongs to karaoke parties — singing is an activity that brings different types of people together.

When you are at church, be sure to sing the hymns with your whole heart. Remember the old saying: "Those who sing, pray twice."

Sing aloud to God our strength; shout for joy to the God of Jacob! Raise a song, sound the timbrel, the sweet lyre with the harp. (Psalm 81:1–2)

Jesus, give me a voice to sing regardless of how I think I sound.

Sheltered From the Wind

In his book, *Mere Christianity*, religious writer C. S. Lewis made an observation worth repeating:

"The real problem of the Christian life comes where people do not usually look for it. It comes the very moment you wake up each morning. All your wishes and hopes for the day rush at you like wild animals. And the first job each morning consists simply in shoving them all back; in listening to that other voice, taking that other point of view, letting that other larger, stronger, quieter life come flowing in.

"And so on, all day. Standing back from all your natural fussings and frettings; coming in out of the wind."

It's a good point. Listen to that other voice carried on the wind. You may catch something you might have missed, something your heart needs to hear.

Wondrously show your steadfast love, O Savior of those who seek refuge from their adversaries at Your right hand. (Psalm 17:7)

Ah, You are lovely, my God!

Making Non-Violent Choices

We usually associate non-violence with Gandhi or Martin Luther King. However, daily opportunities abound for us to make non-violent choices.

Deflect arguments with humor. Take things a little more lightly. Choose not to quarrel. While all difficult situations cannot simply be laughed away, potential problems can be lessened by our willingness to respect the other person – no matter what – as a child of God and to consciously choose not to inflict harm.

Another way to practice non-violence is by carefully selecting our words. Many words in our language suggest violence or are inflammatory. Avoid them.

It's also important to learn to treat ourselves gently. We lessen stress in our lives and make it easier to care for our own spiritual, mental and physical well-being. When we respect, care for and accept ourselves, it is easier to do the same to others.

Finally, the simplest way to be non-violent is to choose to be positive, to be an optimist. Think of problems in terms of solutions, instead of staying stuck in feelings of helplessness, rage and violence.

Those who are hot-tempered stir up strife, but those who are slow to anger calm contention. (Proverbs 15:18)

Lord, give me Your grace to do good.

Legacy of a Bear

A. A. Milne, the English author, once observed that "every one of us hopes secretly for immortality." And he himself wanted to be remembered for his serious literary efforts as a playwright, and as editor and writer for literary magazines.

But as a reviewer remarked, "Man proposes, Pooh disposes."

Milne's four delightful children's books about Winnie the Pooh have appeared in twenty-five languages and several films. Winnie, Eeyore, Tigger and friends are available as toys and appear on clothing.

Few today know of Milne's works for adults, but generations are grateful to the man who brought a little bear to life and gave youngsters a memorable start to their reading lives.

How would you like to be remembered?

Let us work for the good of all. (Galatians 6:10)

Direct our efforts, Holy Spirit, to work for the common good.

Steward and Homemaker

Fatima Traazil, a homemaker from Singapore, says love for her children prompted her to begin an environmental campaign. She realized that otherwise they would inherit many current ecological problems.

Ms. Traazil sets a good example for others. She takes her own cloth shopping bag and reusable containers with her when she shops.

She had environmental pamphlets printed on recycled paper at her own expense. And she bought thousands of biodegradable plastic bags, which she sold to Singaporean shopkeepers for less than they cost her.

She says, "I see my work with the environment as part of my relationship with God and His earth."

Her work is a good reminder that we are all stewards of this earth, wherever we live and whatever we do.

God called the dry land Earth . . . And God saw that it was good. (Genesis 1:10)

May I see Earth's goodness as a reflection, no matter how imperfect, of Your own goodness, Creator.

A Good Scout

Christopher Dean wanted to become an Eagle Scout. That meant he needed a service project.

He also wanted to do something for Marillac House, a shelter for homeless and abused women and children in Salt Lake City, Utah.

So Christopher combined these goals with another personal interest, "I like artwork, so I decided to develop an art exhibit and silent auction that benefit the poor."

He talked with his pastor and the director of Marillac House and obtained a wish list of needed items.

Over a four-month period Christopher arranged for space, managed the advertising, and collected display equipment. Then he contacted artists, artisans and parishioners for donations.

Christopher Dean's art sale netted $6,000 for the shelter.

Volunteer work can take so many different forms. There is so much good waiting to be done. Don't wait to get involved.

One's almsgiving is like a signet-ring with the Lord and He will keep a person's kindness like the apple of His eye. (Sirach 17:22)

Inspire efforts to help the poor and the abused, Father.

Getting Past Discouragement

Physicist Albert Einstein once remarked, "People love chopping wood. In this activity one immediately sees results."

Lots of things we do take years of patient work before we can see any real results.

A tutor or therapist working with a handicapped child must often measure progress in inches instead of miles.

A medical researcher trying to learn the cause of a disease has to explore one avenue after another — and not become discouraged when they turn out to be blind alleys.

Our personal goals may take so long to reach that we get discouraged.

What keeps us from giving up is hope. And hope comes from knowing that we are all important to God, that He will guide our steps — no matter how slow our pace may seem.

If we hope for what we do not see, we wait for it with patience. (Romans 8:25)

Don't let us lose hope, Lord of all hopefulness.

Let There Be Peace

Consider the lovely words of this prayer, first printed in a Boston paper, but appropriate to any city, any town, any neighborhood.

"O God of mercy, understanding and peace, help our beloved city: to maintain racial harmony, to reject all violence, to strive for understanding.

"Let each of us realize our need for You, and our need for one another.

"Let there be peace in our hearts; let there be peace in our city; let this peace begin with me."

If we want to build peaceful cities and a peaceful world where there is racial and ethnic harmony and non-violence we must work to understand and respect each other's common humanity.

We can heal the hate around us — with intelligent, courageous, strong love.

Do good to those who hate you. (Luke 6:27)

Jesus Crucified, make me a respectful and forgiving person, even as I am a respected and forgiven person.

Out of Tune Singer

Most priests and ministers encourage their congregations to join in singing during services. But a priest in San Antonio was forced to seek a court order to stop one member of his congregation from singing.

It seems the woman sang when the choir did – but not the same songs. Instead of joining in the hymns, she sang her own compositions, spoiling the music for everybody else.

Unable to persuade the woman to stop this disruptive singing, the priest finally took the matter to court.

Individuality is vital, but there are times when we must cooperate for the good of everybody. This is true of churches, of nations, of neighborhoods, and certainly of families.

Sing psalms, hymns and spiritual songs to God. (Colossians 3:16)

May the harmony of our songs reflect the harmony of our congregations, families and nations, Holy Spirit.

The Birth of Hans Brinker

After her husband died in 1858, U. S. children's author and editor Mary Mapes Dodge devoted herself to writing and raising her two young sons. Almost every evening she told them stories about Hans Brinker, an adventurous – and fictitious – Dutch lad.

Because her sons enjoyed skating, she wove the stories around a skating competition in which the prize was a pair of silver skates. Her sons loved the stories.

Eventually Mrs. Dodge published them in serial form. And in 1865, she brought the stories out in a book titled *Hans Brinker, or the Silver Skates.* It was so popular that by 1900 some one hundred editions had been published and the book had been translated into six languages.

People familiar with the Netherlands of that period recognized that in the book Mrs. Dodge had given an accurate portrayal of the Dutch countryside, history and life. It was a tribute to her careful research coupled with a careful attention to details she got from her Dutch neighbors. Mrs. Dodge had never been to the Netherlands.

You don't have to be a world traveler to gain an appreciation of other lands and other peoples. Learning is an ongoing process. Every new thing you learn will serve you well at some point.

All wisdom is from the Lord and with Him it remains forever. (Sirach 1:1)

Help me, Holy Spirit, to learn at least one new thing each day about the peoples and countries of our world.

Driver Courtesy Could Be More Common

Common courtesy doesn't seem to be so common anymore, especially on the road. Getting behind the wheel of a car seems to bring out the worst in some people.

You cannot control others, but you can influence them by doing your part and driving carefully and courteously.

Start by maintaining the good condition of your car. Never mix driving with alcohol or drugs. Obey traffic laws and learn to drive defensively. Be sure you and your passengers buckle up.

Remind yourself that this is not the time or place to take out your aggravation and anger on others.

And before you set out on any trip do two things: decide that you won't retaliate if another driver acts foolishly; and say a prayer for yourself and all your neighbors who share the road with you.

Do not return evil for evil. (I Peter 3:9)

Enable drivers to be respectful of themselves and others, Holy Spirit.

Pride: Good and Bad

Pride and self-confidence can be good things. For instance, there is nothing better than a healthy sense of self-respect to protect you from temptation. That, coupled with a love of God, is really the first line of defense against wrongdoing.

But misplaced pride can be a harmful thing. It can keep us from owning up to our faults. The fear of "losing face" can be uncomfortable.

There is a story about a too-cocky youngster who visited a blacksmith. It seems that the smith had just thrown a horseshoe on the ground to cool but the youngster didn't know that.

Out of curiosity, he picked up the hot horseshoe. But, since it burned his fingers, he instantly dropped it.

"Hot, isn't it," the blacksmith observed.

But conscious of the people around, the young fellow replied, "No, no. Not hot really. It's just that it doesn't take me long to look at a horseshoe."

When pride keeps you from admitting your mistakes and taking an honest view of yourself, it's a troublesome thing. Pride is at once the enemy of personal growth and a spur of development. Channel your pride in the right direction.

Pride goes before destruction, and a haughty spirit before a fall. (Proverbs 16:18)

Teach me, Jesus, to channel my pride into life-giving activities.

Formula for Failure

Would you like to be a failure? It's easy. One expert offers this three-step formula.

First, take a dim view of your potential. If you get down on yourself, you'll never recognize the many things you do well.

Second, forget about learning once you get out of school. If you stop learning, you will never have to worry about change and growth.

Finally, assume that you can do everything better by yourself. If you say that you don't need help, you won't get any. Then you can be certain of achieving failure.

If you want to succeed, however, work at developing your potential. Continue to learn every day. Keep abreast of change and be open to growth. And last but not least, try to recognize the help that others can provide — and seek it out.

Work with others and you'll go farther than you ever dreamed possible.

When you come together . . . let all things be done for building up. (I Corinthians 14:26)

Help us assist each other, Holy Lord.

"Only" a Drop in the Ocean

Some problems, like poverty, seem so immense there's a tendency to question the value of one person's contribution. However, Mother Teresa of Calcutta, when asked about the work of her religious community, said, "What we are doing is just a drop in the ocean. But if the drop was not in the ocean, I think the ocean would be less because of the missing drop."

Others have expressed similar sentiments. Lutheran theologian and Biblical scholar, Nobel Peace Prize laureate, musician, medical doctor and missionary, Albert Schweitzer said, "Each of us can do a little to bring some portion of misery to an end."

There are personal rewards in doing each small good deed. Kahlil Gibran wrote: "In the joy of little things the heart finds the morning and is refreshed." Roy Nunley, also a poet, wrote: "Drops of water, grains of sand — with time and unrelenting persistence carve monuments in stone no human effort can match."

Finally, when your efforts seem insignificant, remember the words of St. Madeleine Sophie Barat. "Nothing that can please the heart of our Lord is small."

The kingdom of heaven is like a mustard seed that someone took and sowed in his field; it is the smallest of all the seeds, but when it has grown it is the greatest of shrubs and becomes a tree. (Matthew 13:31–32)

Jesus, remind me daily to love You in small ordinary deeds as well as in great ones.

Disappearing Hometowns and Homes

Each year, as many as two hundred towns in the United States just disappear from the map as far as the Postal Service is concerned.

When a small community's population dwindles, the local post office may close. Residents then receive their mail through the post office of another town.

The loss of their hometown mailing address can be a real blow to a community's sense of identity.

Then there are the many people who literally have no mailing address because they have no homes.

Shelter is a basic human need. But sharing a sense of community, of mattering to others is important, too. Through religious and neighborhood groups, you can reach out to homeless people who otherwise may feel almost invisible to those who pass by — without even looking.

Always seek to do good. (I Thessalonians 5:15)

Compassionate Friend of humankind, how may we extend Your compassion to homeless persons?

Two Special Rings, One Great Difference

When Joe Theismann retired as quarterback for the Washington Redskins in 1985, he ended a record-setting career that brought with it some hard and unexpected lessons.

"I got stagnant," he says. "I thought the team revolved around me. . . . My approach had changed. I was griping about the weather, my shoes, practice times, everything.

"Today I wear my two rings – the winner's ring from Super Bowl XVII and the loser's ring from Super Bowl XVIII. The difference in those two rings lies in applying oneself and not accepting anything but the best."

There's nothing easy about always looking for the best in ourselves. But we owe it to ourselves to live up to our own highest standards every day.

Today, give life your best.

You shall love your neighbor as yourself. (Leviticus 19:18)

Jesus, enable me to love that person hardest to love, myself.

Putting Together
Worker and Work

Quite by accident Esther Cartagena became a one woman job-referral service.

When she worked for the Lower East Side Housing Coalition in New York City, she noticed that many women, like her, had to leave their children alone to attend meetings. They would leave meetings to call to be sure the children were safe.

While she was talking to an unemployed woman, it occurred to her that the woman would welcome work baby-sitting for these women.

When a landlord told her he had to raise a tenant's rent to cover the cost of painting an apartment, she found unemployed neighborhood people to do the job less expensively, so the landlord wouldn't have to raise the rent as much.

Soon new immigrants in the neighborhood started asking Mrs. Cartagena's help in finding work. She tried to help them find jobs in the neighborhood that did not require travel or an extensive knowledge of English.

If you know about job openings or skills training, take the time to tell an unemployed person. Help a needy family find information about food pantries. You can help one person at a time. If you make the extra effort.

Love one another. (I John 3:11)

Jesus, show me how to put love in action today.

Shall I Compare Thee to a Bamboo Shoot?

Bamboo is a very fast growing member of the grass family. A scientist observed one plant grow nearly four feet in twenty-four hours. Some species grow to more than 100 feet tall.

When a particular species does bloom – once every 20 or 120 years – every plant of that species throughout the world flowers at the same time.

In Asian countries bamboo is used for a great variety of things. A suspension bridge with bamboo cables, built across a Chinese river, has been in use for over a thousand years. It's also used for construction scaffolding.

Bamboo is used in Japanese houses for virtually every part not made of paper.

In the United States it is used for fishing rods because of its lightness and flexibility, as well as its unusual strength. It's also used as an ornamental plant.

Bamboo has played an important role in various civilizations because of its particular strengths and properties. That's like you and me. God has given us certain qualities, to fit us for a special role in the world that no one else can fill.

God created humankind in His image, in the image of God He created them; male and female He created them. (Genesis 1:27)

Creator who fashioned me in Your image, help me fill the unique role You have given to me.

Just Short of Perfection

Do you often excuse mistakes — your own or someone else's — by saying "nobody's perfect?" You're right, of course, but that doesn't mean we can't try harder to do the best we can.

What would happen if things were even 99.9% perfect? Consider these possibilities in that remaining one-tenth of one percent:

- 22,000 checks would be deducted from the wrong bank accounts in the next hour.
- 1,312 phone calls would be misplaced in the next minute.
- 2.5 million books would have the wrong covers this year.
- And 315 entries in Webster's dictionary would be misspelled.

Good enough is often not enough. We all make mistakes, but know you've done the very best you can. Avoid perfectionism. Pursue excellence instead.

Commit your work to the Lord, and your plans will be established. (Proverbs 16:3)

Give me the grace, Holy Spirit, to labor toward the fullest use of my gifts and talents.

Grief as Part of Life

At some point in life we are bound to experience a deep grief over the loss of someone dear to us.

Grief can be devastating. Recovery may take a long time. But we are not helpless in the face of grief. Grief can have its positive aspects.

There is an old Chinese proverb that says, "Without sorrows no one becomes a saint." A time of grief can be a period of personal growth.

Edward Marham once wrote, "Only the soul that knows the mighty grief can know the mighty rapture." Grief can help us appreciate the joyous moments that much more.

When grief comes, don't try to run from it. Accept the support of family and friends, cry when you feel the need, but do your best to get on with your life. That's what God wants for you – to live fully each day you have.

He has borne our infirmities and carried our diseases . . . he was wounded for our transgressions, crushed for our iniquities, upon him was the punishment that made us whole, and by his bruises we are healed. (Isaiah 53:4–5)

Thank You, God's Suffering Servant, for taking my weaknesses and sorrows upon Yourself.

Positive Picture of Aging

Marilyn Rhode used to visit her ninety-one-year-old mother-in-law at a convalescent hospital just "long enough to ease my conscience." But then she began to "draw" on the experience.

Rhode, an art teacher in California, started bringing her sketchbook along with her on visits. She sketched portraits of her mother-in-law and also worked on pictures of the woman's friends. Rhode found herself becoming friendly with the women. One woman who had not spoken or shown emotion in months became animated after Rhode did her portrait.

The experience helped Rhode understand the elderly. "I feel like God peeled scales off my eyes. I had not understood older adults," she said. "I fell in love with those I originally feared." She now displays her artwork at colleges and gives speeches and interviews to help others understand the problems of the aged.

You don't have to be an artist to use your creativity to make life better for someone. All you really need are time and desire.

You shall rise before the aged, and defer to the old. (Leviticus 19:32)

Help us accept our own mortality, Jesus, for in that acceptance is born an understanding of those closer to the end of life than the beginning.

What "Letting Go" Means

Here are some simple, though not necessarily easy definitions of "letting go:"

- allowing others to be human, not judging them.
- taking each day as it comes.
- accepting one's self "as is" each day.
- discovering and overcoming personal shortcomings.
- not nagging, scolding or arguing with others about their personal shortcomings.
- living for today and tomorrow, not yesterday.
- allowing others to make their own destinies.

"Letting go" is unclenching our fists, dethroning the idol of our own ego, and, ultimately, seeing ourselves and those around us as God's children. Try it. You'll feel better.

In everything do to others as you would have them do to you; for this is the law and the prophets. (Matthew 7:12)

Jesus, You respect my freedom to accept or reject You. Enable me to extend that same respect to others.

Of Names and Places

Ever wonder how your hometown got its name? Or wonder why some other town's name is Peculiar?

For the people who live in Peculiar, Kansas, it's simple. When townsfolk couldn't agree on a name, a frustrated postal official asked why they kept coming up with such peculiar suggestions.

When another town had trouble coming up with a name, the postmaster looked out the window for inspiration. He didn't see much except grass and shrubs. And that's how Notrees, Texas, got its name.

Sometimes, people decide a name just doesn't seem appropriate or even respectful. When the folks in Mole Hill, West Virginia, felt dissatisfied, what else could they do but turn it into Mountain?

Still, whether it's a town or a person, reputation is really built on how your actions express your character. Give yourself a good name.

Have regard for your name, since it will outlive you longer than a thousand hoards of gold (Sirach 41:12)

Show me what it means to have a good name and how I can preserve it, Holy Spirit.

Age as Incentive to Help Others

Tiofilo Espinoza of Dallas was honored by several local organizations for his contributions to the Hispanic community. Fellow volunteers describe him as reliable and generous.

Espinoza works tirelessly to celebrate Hispanic culture and to help young people by raising money for scholarships.

And he has a special affinity for helping the elderly. He helped found La Voz del Anciano (Voice of the Elderly), which helps senior citizens gain access to services.

Espinoza also happens to be in his nineties.

He says his service to his community is one reason for his longevity. "I made a contract with God when I reached sixty-five years of age," he said. "I told Him: If You give me the strength, I will be here to serve humanity."

One man hasn't let age stop him from helping others who need it. Is something stopping you?

Learn to do good; seek justice, rescue the oppressed, defend the orphan, plead for the widow. (Isaiah 1:17)

Encourage our good deeds, Holy Spirit.

What Goes Around...

A postal clerk in Indianapolis made a discovery about her customers and co-workers — and her own human nature.

A newspaper editorial charged that her branch had "the rudest clerks in town." The clerk was angry.

"I was rude to people because they were rude to me," she said. "What goes around comes around." Then she wondered what would happen if she treated others with courtesy. Would that come around, too?

So, she made an effort to get to know customers' names. The clerk began to smile and ask how they were doing. Even a man known for his grouchiness eventually became a favorite customer. All the clerks began to make an effort. Everybody reaped a reward of cheerfulness.

And it all started with one woman who decided that "what goes around comes around" can be good news.

Show every courtesy to everyone. (Titus 3:2)

May Your courtesy to me remind me to be courteous to others and to my self, God.

Prioritize, Prioritize

Twelve cheerleaders in Ventura, California, squeezed into a Volkswagen as part of a contest. They didn't stay long, though. The car suddenly filled with smoke and forced a hasty exit.

They later found out that the heavy load of their combined weight had pushed the seat springs down against the car's uncovered battery terminals and set fire to the back seat.

Something of this sort can happen when we overload our lives. We become so weighed down by work, activities and commitments that the stress causes emotional burnout.

Learn to set priorities, to decide what's important and what isn't. Simplify your life. Don't let it become so overloaded that the result is harmful physically, emotionally, and spiritually.

Give me neither poverty nor riches; feed me with the food that I need, or I shall be full, and deny you, and say, "Who is the Lord?" or I shall be poor, and steal, and profane the name of my God. (Proverbs 30:8–9)

Give me the wisdom to live temperately, Holy Wisdom.

Your Voiceprint — and Voice — Are Unique

The human voice can now open doors, even without saying, "Open sesame."

Locks that require no keys are opened by the sound of a person's voice. A compact unit with a built-in microphone is installed near the door. The unit is programmed to respond only to the owner's voice. To open the lock, the person punches in an ID number and says a password. In half a second, the unit determines whether the voice is the right one, and if it is, opens the door.

What makes this sort of lock workable and secure is that people's voices are as individual as fingerprints. No one trying to imitate the owner's voice will be able to fool the unit, because individual voice patterns can not be duplicated. It also won't respond to a recording; it can distinguish a real voice from a recorded one.

However, the person whose voice sounds differently because of a cold or the like, is in no danger of being locked out. Distinctive voice patterns remain.

Your voice is always important. Words of encouragement can open new vistas of hope for a friend.

Let your unique voice be used by the Holy Spirit as an instrument of love.

The Spirit of the Lord speaks through me, His word is upon my tongue. (2 Samuel 23:2)

God, may my words reflect Your will.

Listening Heart-to-Heart

This story was told more than seven centuries ago by the Persian poet Attar:

A sick man was weeping bitterly. Someone went up to him and asked, "Why are you crying?"

The sick man answered, "I am crying to attract the pity of God's heart."

The other said, "You're talking nonsense, for God doesn't have a physical heart."

The sick man replied, "It's you who are wrong. He is the owner of all the hearts that exist. It's through the heart that you can make your connection with God."

This story's message still speaks to people of all faiths. When our hearts are open to the needs of others we can become the instrument of God's help to them.

Cries for help take many forms. We often have to listen for the feeling behind a person's words or behavior. A friend or family member who lashes out with angry words for no apparent reason may be saying, "Things are rough for me right now, and the pain is more than I can cope with." A child who misbehaves may be trying to get attention because he or she feels neglected.

Become a channel for God's love.

O Lord my God, I cried to You for help, and You have healed me. O Lord, You have brought up my soul from Sheol. (Psalm 30:2–3)

That I might be privileged to be Your heart for someone in distress of mind, soul and body, God!

Lincoln Took His Medicine

Abraham Lincoln had many qualities worth imitating, including his appreciation of humor. He clearly understood laughter's healing power.

One day in 1862, he called his closest advisors to a meeting. They found Lincoln engrossed in a book. He started to read aloud to them. Lincoln found the humorous piece very funny but none of the others laughed along with him.

"Why don't you laugh?" he asked. "With the fearful strain that is upon me night and day, if I did not laugh I should die, and you need this medicine as much as I do."

Then, getting to work, he shared with them what he called "a little paper of much significance" that he had drafted: the Emancipation Proclamation.

Judgment and creativity need humor for balance. The greater your daily burden, the more you need to laugh.

But let the righteous be joyful; let them exult before God; let them be jubilant with joy. (Psalm 68:3)

Preserve us from humorlessness, Jesus.

Inventing the Future

Elijah McCoy, the son of a slave who fled to Canada, perfected a device to oil moving locomotives, leading to the expression "the real McCoy."

Norbert Rillieux's developments in vacuum evaporation made the production of refined sugar economically feasible.

C. J. Walker began as a washerwoman and ended as a self-made millionaire. She developed and successfully promoted a line of beauty products as well as a product for straightening the hair of black women.

In 1914, Garrett Morgan invented a safety hood to protect fire fighters.

The contributions of these and other Black American inventors have improved the lives of their fellow citizens.

Each race, each ethnic group, each religious group, contributes much to make our country better today than yesterday, and better tomorrow than today.

The memory of the righteous is a blessing. (Proverbs 10:7)

Enlighten me, Spirit of the Living God.

Happy Valentine's Day

Valentine's Day shouldn't be the only day you tell your loved ones how you feel. Here are some ideas on how to say "I love you" year-round.

- Share vegetables from your garden with your neighbors.
- Invite someone to watch the sunset with you.
- Pick out a quality you admire in someone, and let them know it.
- Call or write former teachers or mentors and tell them how much they helped you.
- Donate blood.
- Make an effort to welcome a new person at work, church, or the neighborhood.
- Leave love notes for your family on the bathroom mirror, the refrigerator or TV, inside a lunchbox.
- Bury the hatchet, and forgive someone.

Learn to love others, as God loves you. And show that love every day of the year.

As I have loved you, you also should love one another. (John 13:34)

Jesus, thanks for Your loving touch.

The Courage of Her Convictions

The Civil Rights movement owes much to the courage of one woman: Rosa Parks. In 1955, she refused to give up her seat on the bus to a white man. The event sparked protests and boycotts which led to the Supreme Court ruling that racial segregation is unconstitutional.

"I have learned over the years that knowing what must be done does away with fear," she said later.

"When I sat down on the bus that day, I had no idea history was being made – I was only thinking of getting home. But I had made up my mind . . . I did not feel any fear sitting there. I felt the Lord would give me the strength to endure whatever I had to face.

"It was time for someone to stand up – or in my case, sit down. So I refused to move."

Let God guide you in living a life filled with courage.

I am continually with You; You hold my right hand. You guide me with Your counsel, and afterward You will receive me with honor. (Psalm 73:23–24)

Help us live according to sound values, Lord.

The Gift of Hope

At a time when political and economic conditions in the Czech Republic were somewhat difficult, the nation's president, Vaclav Havel, said in a speech:

"I . . . carry hope in my heart. Hope is a feeling that life and work have meaning. You either have it or you don't, regardless of the state of the world around you. Life without hope is an empty, boring, and useless life. I cannot imagine that I could strive for something if I did not carry hope in me. I am thankful to God for this gift. It is as big a gift as life itself."

When we find ourselves in difficult circumstances, our hope can sustain us – the hope that comes from knowing that life has meaning, that God loves us and is always with us to help us carry our burdens.

God so loved the world that He gave His only Son, so that everyone who believes in Him may not perish but may have eternal life. (John 3:16)

Thank You, Father, for the gift of Your Son.

Dream Becomes Reality

Jean Forman had wanted to be a doctor for as long as she could remember. But she had delayed college to start a family.

She decided to enroll in college at age forty. With encouragement from her family, she graduated from the University of Southern California School of Medicine at the age of fifty-one, becoming the oldest student to earn a degree from the school.

Dr. Forman's next goal: becoming a family physician. She said, "We each have one lifetime to do something with. Even if I had not made it to medical school, at least I would know that I tried. If I had not, I would have always wondered, 'What if?'"

Everybody has goals and dreams that can be accomplished only with effort. It's easy to keep putting things off. But if you get to work on making your dream a reality, you will never have to ask yourself, "What if?"

I will pour out My Spirit on all flesh; your sons and your daughters shall prophesy . . . dream dreams, and . . . see visions. (Joel 2:28)

Lord of the prophetesses and prophets of every age, fill me with Your Spirit.

Corrosion and Self-Destruction

Books printed before the middle of the nineteenth century endured many hundreds of years. Today's books self-destruct after fifty years or so.

The reason is changes in papermaking. Chemicals now used in the process leave an acid residue that gradually corrodes the paper.

In our lives, there is an equally corrosive effect when we harbor anger and resentment. Holding a grudge against someone who has wronged us destroys our physical, emotional, and spiritual well-being. It literally eats us up.

There are times when it's natural to feel anger or resentment, but we can get rid of these negative emotions through forgiveness. Forgiveness not only frees others from the destructive effect of our ill will, it frees us as well.

Peter [asked], . . . "how often should I forgive? As many as seven times?" Jesus said to him, "Not seven times, but . . . seventy-seven times."
(Matthew 18:21–22)

Forgiving Lord, enable me to forgive.

You Have a Mission

The Christopher message that the individual has enormous potential for good goes all over the world. A reminder of that came in a letter from a Hindu religious teacher.

This man is a member of a Hindu monastic community that lives in a secluded forest in India. And yet our message had reached him there.

In his letter, he said, "How right you are when you say that each one of us has a different mission in life and that each of us should strive to fulfill it. That is exactly what I have been doing here since I came to this forest."

Discover your mission in life. Carry it out. And then, whether you live in a forest, a village or a city; whatever your marital or economic status, you will have happiness.

There is happiness in living your mission – in living out God's will for you.

The ordinances of the Lord are true and righteous. (Psalm 19:9)

Lead me, Lord, in the way You would have me go.

Caring Is Catching On

A Norwalk, Connecticut, mother was concerned because the hallways of her son's high school were dingy and unattractive. Budget cuts made it impossible for the school to paint them. But Nan Haavik refused to believe it could not be done.

She organized parents to paint the halls. Since union regulations didn't allow volunteers to do maintenance painting, the parents made the paint job decorative — adding sports, art, and music symbols along the walls. They worked during team and band practice to avoid the cost of keeping the building open after hours.

The number of volunteers grew and the school got a thorough refurbishing.

Mrs. Haavik says, "I just try to . . . show the world somebody cares. It's contagious."

A man was going down from Jerusalem to Jericho, and he fell among robbers . . . But a Samaritan . . . came to where he was; and . . . had compassion. (Luke 10:30, 33)

I pray that I might be compassionate, God.

On Compromise and Planning

Good choices take long-term consideration into account.

For years after the Revolutionary War, Congress was at an impasse about whether the federal government should assume the war debts of states and about where the nation's capital should be located.

In a compromise, Southerners agreed to the debt measure. Northerners agreed that the capital would be in Philadelphia for ten years. Then it would be moved to a site on the Potomac favored by President Washington. He envisioned the river as an important shipping route.

Washington's choice of a swampy wilderness area was unpopular. Congressmen called it "wilderness city" and "a mud hole." But in time, his vision for the District of Columbia was realized.

Many worthwhile things take time. In some cases even beyond our own lifetimes. Don't let discouragement or shortsightedness stop you.

Mighty King, lover of justice, You have established equity; You have executed justice and righteousness. (Psalm 99:4)

Show us how to work for justice even when we know we shall not see the results in our own lifetimes, Jesus.

Conflict and Resolution

Here are some ideas that will help you resolve conflicts when they arise:

- Don't delay too long before you act.
- Be sure no one is being misquoted or misinterpreted.
- See the dispute as a problem to be resolved together.
- Be fully informed about the issue.
- Build on even minor areas of agreement.
- Explore various solutions.
- Resolve to seek the common good.
- If needed, seek the help of a neutral party.

If you approach conflicts with intelligence and good will, they become easier to resolve without injuring others or building resentment. Managing conflict is an important step on the road to peace.

Come to terms quickly with your accuser while you are on the way to court with him. (Matthew 5:25)

Show me how to avoid arguments and solve conflicts, Prince of Peace.

Talking It Out

Talk, it is said, is cheap. And that is true, as far as it goes. But talk is also a remarkable human characteristic.

Talk teaches. Talk encourages. Talk comforts. Talk leads. Talk heals. Talk shows respect for others. Talk relieves tensions. Talk can even help resolve disputes.

When two people disagree, they will stay right where they are if they don't talk about their disagreement. People have to talk with each other if they wish to sort out their differences, if they wish to find a common ground enabling them to begin the process of reconciliation.

So whenever a problem in human relations arises, try talking about it. Give others a chance to talk, too. Remember to talk with someone, not at them.

And, above all, listen to each other. That's the hard part. Talk can do all of the good things mentioned above and more. Or it can exacerbate the situation. How we talk — and listen — is our choice.

I must speak . . . I must open my lips and answer. (Job 32:20)

Open my lips to speak, my ears to hear, Creator.

Visitors Clog Mountain's Trails

Crowding, a fact of contemporary life, is a relative term. At 20,306 feet, Mt. McKinley, in Denali National Park, is the highest peak in North America. More than a thousand people come in May and June just to attempt the climb.

The paths to Mt. McKinley during these two months are nearing peak traffic load — 383 people on the mountain at one time.

People come from all over the world to try the arduous, dangerous climb. Often, their goal is invisible behind mists and clouds. But still they come.

They bring with them that hallmark of civilization, litter. Climbing gear, cans, packages, equipment, all are forgotten, lost or just discarded, despite strict National Park Service rules.

Since not everybody obeys the rules, park officials are asking climbers for advice on better managing crowds and the problems they bring.

Whether you are alone or part of a crowd, plan for potential problems. Then, be part of the solution.

Happy is the person who meditates on wisdom . . . pursuing her like a hunter, and lying in wait on her paths. (Sirach 14:20, 22)

Holy Spirit, enlighten me that I may indeed be part of the solution to various problems.

Learning to Serve

Students at some of New York City's private schools are engaged in volunteer community service. They tutor other students in need of special help or work in soup kitchens or shelters for the homeless.

One student sees community service as a means of building bridges between groups.

Another student says, "I don't know if the world can really be changed. But one on one, I can make people a little happier, and that's a step in the right direction."

Many of us may feel that what we can do is limited. But if we each do a little to increase understanding and to help others, together we can change the world.

Be courageous and valiant. (2 Samuel 13:28)

Please give me a share of Your courage and Your love for all people, Crucified Jesus.

Sticky Question

Few people heard of George de Mestral. The Swiss-born inventor died in February, 1990 and his obituary was on the back pages of newspapers, if at all.

He received his first patent at age twelve, and spent years perfecting the fastener we know as Velcro. The name is a combination of, "velvet" and "crochet," the latter a French word for "hook." Velcro fasteners are made of two strips of nylon, one consisting of tiny loops, the other covered with tiny hooks.

When pressed together, the strips cling to each other, much as thistle burrs cling to clothing. In fact it was a walk in the woods in 1941 that led to the development of Velcro. De Mestral came out of the wooded area outside of Geneva with burrs sticking to his clothing and wondered why.

After seven years of research, he knew. Today Velcro is used to fasten everything from clothing to artificial hearts and the manufacturer says it will still hold fast after being fastened as much as fifty thousand times.

"Why?," one of the most provocative words in any language, is the mark of an inquisitive mind. The inquisitive mind is behind the progress of civilization.

Never be afraid to ask why, to probe, to reason.

Ask, and it will be given you; search, and you will find; knock, and the door will be opened to you. (Matthew 7:7)

Bless me with an inquisitive mind, Creator.

Put Healthy Guilt to Work

What is guilt?

A simple definition is that guilt is the unpleasant feeling we have when we are aware of having done something wrong, or have left undone something right.

So guilt can be a warning. Or guilt can be an indication that we feel we have fallen short of our own impossible standards. Trying to ignore guilt feelings, psychologists say, won't make them go away.

Instead, when you are feeling guilty, take a few moments to think about the cause. If something is wrong, how can you correct it? Do it. Then leave the guilt in the past. If you're imposing perfectionism on yourself, it's time to reevaluate.

This frees you to be the good person you have the potential to be. There is nothing so refreshing as a clear conscience.

Christ Jesus came into the world to save sinners. (I Timothy 1:15)

Thank You, Jesus, for saving me from sin and guilt that is inappropriate.

Feeling Special, Doing Better

One man in Miami is trying to keep kids off the streets — and on the playing fields.

Roberto Riva created the Allapattah Jaguars sports club, with ten teams for boys and girls. He also bought uniforms and equipment as well as arranging for free physical examinations.

People in the struggling neighborhood feel that Riva's actions will give kids a positive outlook. "When you live in a place like this and everybody says so many bad things about the area, you start feeling there is something wrong with you," said Father José Menendez, pastor of Corpus Christi Church. "But when somebody comes from outside and says, 'No. You are special. So special that I'm going to become involved in your life and try to help,' that for us is an inspiration."

There isn't one person on earth who couldn't and doesn't benefit from being inspired by another's goodness. Or by being the one who is doing the inspiring.

If you . . . know how to give good gifts to your children, how much more will the heavenly Father give the Holy Spirit to those who ask Him! (Luke 11:13)

Father, inspire me to be caring and compassionate in practical ways.

Time – Past, Present, Future

In early societies, people didn't need to know the exact time. They began work at sunrise and stopped at sunset. But as the complexity of civilization grew, so did the need for measuring time accurately.

Sundials were used in ancient Egypt, Greece and Rome. So were water clocks. These bowls, wide on top and narrow at the bottom, were marked with hours. They were filled with water that leaked out a hole at the bottom.

The fourteenth century saw the first mechanical clock. This clock used movable weights and a notched wheel and varied about fifteen minutes a day. Timekeeping improved markedly in the seventeenth century. First came the pendulum clock – accurate to ten seconds a day. Then came the balance wheel clock operated by a spring – accurate to one-third second a day.

This century brought the quartz clock, in which a small piece of quartz vibrates when an alternating electric current is applied. The best of these vary only a millisecond a month. The National Bureau of Standards atomic clock is accurate to one second in 370,000 years.

While we need to measure time, obsession with it keeps us from experiencing the uniqueness of each moment. Take time out. Stop worrying about your schedule and start thinking about something bigger – eternity.

For everything there is a season, and a time for every matter. (Ecclesiastes 3:l)

Holy Spirit, may I enter fully into each moment of this day.

Turning a Foreign Phrase

If you have the chance to travel in foreign countries, one of the problems — and delights — of hearing other languages is interpreting idioms. Just as in English, we say "It's raining cats and dogs," in France it comes down in ropes; in Spain, in jugs; and in Italy, water basins.

Every language has its own wonderful way with words. French seems especially preoccupied with food and drink. The equivalent of turning up like a bad penny is arriving like a hair in the soup. We might say knee-high to a grasshopper. In France the comparison is as tall as three apples.

Throughout history, people have transformed language into something of charm and beauty. Unfortunately, words are also capable of causing great harm.

Try to speak the way you'd like to be spoken to.

Whoever listens to you listens to Me.
(Luke 10:16)

Let me remember, Jesus, that our voices are the ones others hear.

Looney Cartoons Are Serious Work

Animated cartoons, which look like simple drawings, are not simple to produce. A story is sketched on storyboards. Then animators do a series of drawings, each showing a slight change in the position of figures to bring characters to life and make them "move."

A recording is made of actors reading their lines. The words are divided into sounds and written on an exposure sheet, to show with what frames they are to be synchronized.

Making a character say "Good morning, how are you?" takes over two dozen drawings just to produce the mouth movements. One minute of action can require as many as one thousand drawings. Computers now do some of the "in-between" images.

Drawings are traced on transparent sheets or electronically copied, then individually colored. Each one is photographed over painted backgrounds — 1440 frames of film for each minute. Finally, film and sound tracks are combined, finishing the incredibly detailed work.

In real life, too, most goals are achieved by one small, painstaking effort after another. They may seem to do little, but their sum total can be a spectacular achievement.

Be steadfast and do not be impetuous in time of calamity. Cling to Him. . . . Accept whatever befalls upon you, and in times of humiliation be patient. (Sirach 2:2–4)

Give me patient fidelity come what may, Lord.

Family Writes Rules for Survival

After the death of a woman who was both wife and mother, her family, struggling with major changes as well as grief, composed these "Rules of Survival":

Thou shalt be considerate at all times.

Thou shalt respect other's rights, privileges, sensibilities, freedom and privacy.

Thou shalt put thy clothes where they belong and shalt not clutter . . . but that which thou does in thy own room shall not be the business of others unless it infringes on their rights.

That which thou takest out, thou shalt put back.

Thou shalt not take that which does not belong to thee without asking.

Thou shalt do thy share of the work.

Thou shalt not waste heat, hot water, electricity.

Thou shalt give advance notice of thy comings and goings if (they) . . . will keep thee away at mealtime.

Thou shalt not criticize others in the house, nor ridicule their views, nor prolong a dispute.

The list ended with this observation: "If we try to live by the spirit of these rules, this will continue to be a happy home, whatever difficulties beset us."

What rules govern life in your household, your family relationships?

If you wish to enter into life, keep the Commandments. (Matthew 19:17)

O that we might rejoice to keep Your commandments, Lord of the Covenant!

Two Good Neighbors

Barbara Williams and Bill Ogburn live three thousand miles apart. They don't know each other, but they have something wonderful in common.

Barbara Williams is a security guard at P.S. 94 in the Bronx, New York. For almost twenty years she has greeted parents and students, encouraging them to be on time and to talk about school and family problems. She offers understanding and practical help, like information on jobs or babysitting. In a neighborhood that knows poverty, drugs and violence, Barbara Williams gives comfort and stability.

Bill Ogburn is one of a now rare breed. He is a milkman who has delivered good cheer to his customers in Los Angeles for over forty years. He brings groceries to older folks who find it hard to get out. He even offers credit to those who have trouble paying their bill. He says of his customers, "I have a lot of great folks."

Bill Ogburn and Barbara Williams are experts at loving their neighbors. They are also examples for every one who would like to be a good neighbor, too.

Jesus answered . . . "You shall love your neighbor as yourself." (Mark 12:29–31)

Man of Nazareth, help me fulfill the second great commandment.

Knowing Your Place
in the Universe

These days more and more of us are considering the environment and our place in it. We are asking about our responsibilities, about what we can do and where we fit in.

These words are from a sixteenth century Irish cleric who saw himself as part of the whole universe even as he prayed for his own soul.

"Holy God," he prayed, "I entreat Thee by water. . . . I entreat Thee by earth. . . . I entreat Thee by every human creature that ever tasted death and life. I entreat Thee by time with its clear divisions. I entreat Thee by darkness. I entreat Thee by the light. I entreat all the elements in heaven and earth – that the eternal sweetness may be granted to my soul."

God wants us to appreciate His universe, just as He wants us to desire His eternity. Take some of God's precious time to contemplate your place in His Holy plan.

Long ago You laid the foundation of the earth; and the heavens are the work of Your hands. (Psalm 102:25)

Remind me, Creator, that I am a steward of all that You created. Help me understand my role now – and in my life to come.

Learning Real Value

Discussing family money problems with children is difficult. Pride and a sense of failure and loss get in the way.

Children usually know what's up. The crisis can be an opportunity to teach children about thrift, discipline, action-taking and the way a family works.

It is important for children to be involved, to be made aware of the problem, but not made to feel somehow responsible for solving it.

Being sensitive to your children's questions will help you know how much they are capable of understanding. Be specific. Explain the problem and how the family will deal with it. Ask the children for ways they might help.

Even small children can make contributions, and should be shown and told that these count. Although an older child's willingness to contribute, perhaps by getting a part time job, may be useful, let youngsters know that money is not the only way to help. Emotional support to weather rough times can be as valuable as dollars.

Relationships are still the most important things in life.

All who believed . . . had all things in common; they would sell their possessions and goods and distribute the proceeds to all, as any had need. (Acts 2:44–45)

Holy One, guide us that we may work together in solving family problems in the spirit of Your law of love.

Growth of Love

After visiting famed horticulturist Luther Burbank, Helen Keller said of him:

"When plants talk to him he listens. That is why they tell him so many things about themselves. . . . Mr. Burbank feels the individuality . . . of the plant . . . so he encourages the plant to put forth the best of which it is capable."

When Burbank was asked how he could keep track of details about his thousands of plants, he replied: "I do it with love. I feel an affection for everything I am working with, and so I can keep in touch with everything that concerns them."

Just as plants respond to care and sensitivity to their individual needs, so children blossom when they receive love and appreciation. They need words of encouragement to let them know that they are special and important.

Help the youngsters in your home, in your town, to flourish, to blossom.

Can a woman forget her nursing child, or show no compassion for the child of her womb? Even these may forget, yet I will not forget you. See, I have inscribed you on the palms of My hands. (Isaiah 49:15–16)

That I might never forget Your compassion, Abba. That I may show it to your children.

Keep Lent Well

Robert Herrick, a seventeenth century poet, has some good advice as we begin Lent.

"Is this a fast, to keep / The larder lean? / And clean / From fat of veals, and sheep? / Is it to quit the dish / of flesh, yet still / To fill / The platter high with fish? / Is it to fast an hour, / Or ragged to go, / Or show a downcast look, and sour? /

"No: 'tis a fast, to dole / Thy sheaf of wheat, and meat / Unto the hungry soul. / It is to fast from strife, / From old debate / And hate; / To circumcise thy life./

"To show a heart grief-rent; / To starve thy sin, / not bin; / And that's to keep thy Lent."

Though over three hundred years old, Herrick's advice is still fresh today. Follow it. Keep a Lent full of mercy and humility.

Return to Me with all your heart, with fasting, with weeping, and with mourning; rend your hearts and not your clothing. (Joel 2:12–13)

God, enable me to keep a Lent of justice and mercy, kindness and humility, prayerfulness — and joy.

An Evening Prayer

Most of us are used to speaking to God in our own words. But at times, traditional prayers, including prayers from other faiths or backgrounds, can enhance our reflections.

Rev. William Kolb of Calvary Episcopal Church in Memphis has a special feeling for this ancient prayer which is said at the end of the day. He finds in it a reminder that "Ours is a God of compassion for 'all sorts and conditions' of humankind. . . . And we need God to help us remain sensitively and caringly aware of the suffering of others."

Here then is the beautiful prayer:

Keep watch, dear Lord, with those who work, or watch, or weep this night, and give Thine angels charge over those who sleep. Tend the sick, Lord Christ; give rest to the weary, bless the dying, soothe the suffering, pity the afflicted, shield the joyous; and all for Thy love's sake. Amen.

Again, Amen.

Come, bless the Lord, all you servants of the Lord, who stand by night in the house of the Lord! (Psalm 134:1)

Lord Christ, be our shelter and lamp during the hours of darkness.

The Things We Know
– But Don't

How many times along the spiritual road do we find ourselves saying, "I know, I know?" Things we learned early in life, are offered to us as solutions to our problems: "Turn it over to God." "Your will, not mine, be done." "Pray." "Do unto others." "Forgive."

But, we think, "I already know all that."

It is difficult to hear another when we believe we have all the answers already. Or to accept the fact that maybe someone else can add more insight, can be more objective.

Humility is required to listen, to ask for help and really mean it, to be willing to do it someone else's way, or to say, "I don't know. My way hasn't worked."

Often, when we become willing to truly listen, to hear anew something we've heard before, we find a certain kind of clarity and a fresh perspective.

Amazingly, it sometimes happens that when we turn outwards, when we listen to what others are trying to tell us, we are suddenly graced once again with the power to look within and find the answers that have eluded us.

I have taught you the way of wisdom; I have led you in the paths of uprightness. . . . Keep hold of instruction, do not let go; guard her, for she is your life. (Proverbs 4:11, 13)

Give me wisdom, Lord, and courage to listen and to act.

Art of Self-Restraint

We often speak of acting out of thoughtfulness and kindness. But sometimes it's just as essential not to act too quickly.

Arthur Conan Doyle, author of the Sherlock Holmes tales, recounted this incident from his friendship with writer George Meredith: "The nervous complaint from which he suffered caused him to fall down occasionally. As we walked up the narrow path I heard him fall behind me, but judged from the sound that it was a mere slither and could not have hurt him. Therefore I walked on as if I had heard nothing. He was a fiercely proud old man and my instincts told me that his humiliation in being helped would be far greater than any relief I could give him."

It's hard to restrain ourselves when our first reaction is to do something. Yet, there are times when the best thing to do is nothing.

The commandments . . . are summed up in this word, love your neighbor as yourself. . . . love is the fulfilling of the law. (Romans 13:9–10)

Holy Spirit, how may I be tactful and charitable?

Cooperating with God

Here's a quote worth contemplating from George Eliot's poem Stradivarius: "'Tis God gives skill, but not without man's hands. He could not make Antonio Stradivari's violins without Antonio."

In order to use our God-given gifts well we need to recognize our potential. And that means appreciating — and developing — our gifts and our strengths. It demands that we overcome limitations and imbalances.

It also means remembering that we are made in God's image and likeness.

Listen to the Master. Turn His gifts into a full life lived gently, reverently, purposefully.

It was You who formed my inward parts; You knit me together in my mother's womb. I praise You, for I am fearfully and wonderfully made. (Psalm 139:1, 13–14)

Thank You, Father, for making me Your co-worker.

Likes, Dislikes and You

There's someone close to you that you may not be too crazy about. And that's a real shame.

"Most people do not like themselves at all," wrote Pulitzer Prize-winning novelist John Steinbeck. "They distrust themselves, put on masks and pomposities. They quarrel and boast and pretend and are jealous because they do not like themselves.

"If we could learn to like ourselves even a little, maybe our cruelties and angers might melt away. Maybe we would not have to hurt one another just to keep our ego chins above water."

Even if we don't act in all those negative ways, there's probably more than a little truth here.

Try looking at yourself the way God and your best friend would: recognize your faults, yes. But enjoy and celebrate all the good qualities that make you – you.

You shall love your neighbor as yourself. (Matthew 19:19)

Creator, how marvelously You've made me!

Friends of Youth Lend Support

When thirteen-year-old Mark Lowy of Illinois found out that he had leukemia, he also found that he had lots of friends.

Mark's schoolmates learned that he was going to be starting chemotherapy treatments which would probably cause him to lose his hair.

To give him moral support, the other seventh and eighth-grade boys at his school decided to shave their heads so that he wouldn't feel different.

Mark thought it was great, but since he was just starting chemotherapy, his hair hadn't been affected yet. Within a week, Mark was just about the only boy who wasn't bald. His sympathetic schoolmates had rushed ahead to do their good deed.

There are lots of ways to show others we care. Sometimes, we need to act fast. Sometimes, we need to make plans. In either case, don't let opportunity for good pass you by.

Some friends play at friendship but a true friend sticks closer than one's nearest kin. (Proverbs 18:24)

Give us genuine friends, Divine Friend.

The Tides of Change

Janet Zeller's painful and progressive neurological disease, Reflex Sympathetic Disorder, threatened the active outdoor lifestyle she knew and loved.

Within a year, the Dunbarton, New Hampshire, native was a quadriplegic. She lost her job. Her husband walked out. She fought despair and prayed for peace, strength and guidance.

With help, she created a special kayak to compensate for her disabilities and began canoeing and kayaking. Janet Zeller became an instructor, and was asked by the American Canoe Association (ACA) to introduce handicapped paddlers to the sport.

Elected national president of the ACA, she started recreational programs for the disabled. "I want to do as much as I can, while I can," she says. "God has shown me my life has a purpose, and with his help, I've reaped the benefits."

With confidence in God and yourself, you can achieve anything.

I am your God, I will strengthen you, I will help you. (Isaiah 41:10)

Lord, give me strength to do things I would never attempt on my own.

Honesty — and a Second Chance

Tom and Pauline Nichter of California were homeless and jobless when they found a wallet containing a large amount of cash. Rather than taking the money for themselves, the Nichters returned the wallet to its rightful owner.

They were rewarded for their honesty.

The local police gave them $300 and strangers sent donations. An elderly couple gave them a check for $2,400 — the amount that was in the wallet.

The couple, who had been out of work for a year, were about to give up hope when all of this happened. They were overwhelmed by the kindness of strangers.

As Pauline Nichter said, "I can't believe this. All we did was what we were brought up to do — to be honest. We're getting our second chance, and God, it feels good."

Honesty is not a quality of character that becomes disposable in hard times. If you are a person of integrity it is who you are and how you live everyday.

Trust in the Lord, and do good; so you will live in the land, and enjoy security. (Psalm 37:3)

I want to turn from all that keeps us apart, Savior. Make me the person You want me to be.

Hymn to the Treasure of Your Heart

An eighth century Irish hymn offers thoughts worth pondering – and living.

> Be Thou my vision, O Lord of my heart . . .
> Be Thou my best thought in the day and night . . .
> Be Thou my wisdom . . .
> Be Thou my great Father, and I Thy true child . . .
> Be Thou my breastplate, my sword for the fight;
> Be Thou my whole armor, be Thou my true might . . .
> Be Thou my soul's shelter, be Thou my strong tower . . .
> Be Thou mine inheritance now and always . . .
> Be Thou and Thou only the first in my heart.

If we try to live these words, we can truly sing with all our souls, "O Sovereign of heaven, my treasure Thou art."

"You are my Lord; I have no good apart from You." . . . The Lord is my chosen portion and my cup . . . the boundary lines have fallen for me in pleasant places; I have a goodly heritage. (Psalm 16:2, 5–6)

Thank You for Your companionship, Lord, my delight and my inheritance.

Old Answers to Violence

The metal detector used at airports today isn't really a modern invention. In the third century B.C. a Chinese emperor used a metal detector to guard his palace.

Emperor Chin Shih Huang Ti is best known for building the Great Wall to keep out the Mongols from Central Asia. He also built a spacious palace complex which he seldom left.

As protection against assassins, he had a special magnetite door installed. When anyone wearing armor or carrying weapons came to the door, the armor or weapon was attracted by the magnetite and the person was prevented from entering.

Today's metal detectors are more sophisticated, but then so are the weapons.

The age-old problem of violence needs to be faced today, starting with the abundance of weapons in homes and communities. This isn't just a matter for law-makers. Make your opinion known. Be willing to work for peace.

Destruction and violence are before me; strife and contention arise. (Habakkuk 1:3)

Dear God, when will we end violence, strife and contention?

Here's to Somebody

Here's a story you may have heard before. It's about four people named Everybody, Somebody, Anybody, and Nobody.

There was an important job to do in the organization to which they all belonged. Everybody was asked to do it. Everybody was sure that Somebody would do it.

In reality, Anybody could have done it. But Nobody did it. Somebody got angry about that because it was Everybody's job.

Nobody realized that Everybody wouldn't do it. It ended up with Everybody blaming Somebody. That meant that Nobody could really blame Anybody.

Sound familiar? You can give it a different ending. All you have to do is decide that you want to be Somebody. If you do not do your job, who will?

The people did the work faithfully.
(2 Chronicles 34:12)

Carpenter from Nazareth, help me to work with care.

Moderation Makes the Difference

Salt is essential to human life even though it's composed of poisonous chlorine and sodium.

Our bodies can not function without salt. We have special taste buds just for it, and we crave it. If we lose too much salt through perspiration or certain medicines, we can become seriously ill.

Yet too much salt can raise blood pressure to dangerous levels in sensitive individuals or in those with certain medical conditions.

So the key to our consumption of salt is balance and moderation.

The same is true of many other things that affect health. Too much alcohol, food, or stress can damage our well-being.

Freeing ourselves from excesses and addictions of any kind can be difficult. Don't be afraid to get professional help. And don't be afraid to turn your problems over to God in prayer.

In everything you do be moderate, and no sickness will overtake you. (Sirach 31:22)

Let me trust You in all things, Lord God. You want the best for me, even more than I do myself.

Enjoying the Here and Now

Around this time of year, Egyptians celebrate a holiday called Sham al-Nessim, the Smelling of Spring. Egyptian families spend the day outdoors, picnicking and enjoying the fresh spring air. A family might go to a park or a desert oasis or on a riverboat excursion. There are games, singing, story-telling, and kite-flying for the children. The purpose is simply to enjoy the beauty of the season, of the earth, of the day.

This could serve as an example. Our holidays and vacations are often so hectic that we don't enjoy them.

On Thanksgiving Day we spend so much time and effort preparing mountains of food that we are thankful when the day is over. At Christmas we are caught in a whirl of shopping for gifts, decorating, entertaining and being entertained. Often we are too rushed and preoccupied to experience the real joy of season.

Vacations become marathons, planned to cover maximum territory in minimum time. Instead of coming back refreshed, we are likely to return exhausted.

Don't let plans and an overcrowded schedule push aside the present. Take time to relax, to savor the fragrance of flowers, the warmth of the sun-light, the sound of laughter. The joy of the moment is God's gift to us.

Great are the works of the Lord, studied by all who delight in them. (Psalm 111:2)

Slow me down, Lord, that I may appreciate the present.

Not a Dog-Eat-Dog World

"Scientists have long been mystified as to why anyone would ever do something unselfish for anyone else," says writer Thomas Bass. "These displays of niceness don't seem to square with the Darwinian scheme of things." According to that theory, the strongest grab all the food they can. Animals that share should die out.

But they haven't. Some animals such as chimpanzees share food — not just with relatives but with other members of their group.

Two Austrian mathematicians used computer simulation to study behavior strategies. They found that in the long run, animals that exploit others will be the ones to die out. Unselfish ones that share food and information will flourish.

Not a bad reminder that needing others and looking out for others is not only good, it's natural.

Do not reach out your hand for everything you see. . . . Judge your neighbor's feelings by your own, and in every matter be thoughtful. (Sirach 31:14–15)

Jesus, enable me to be unselfish.

Being Attentive to Others

Nick Goodall was considered one of the greatest violinists of the nineteenth century, but he was so eccentric that he never achieved fame.

He once began a concert tour, but it ended with the first performance. The house was packed and the audience enthralled by his brilliant playing. The problem came when it was time for the concert to end. He kept playing . . . and playing. As the night wore on, the tired audience gradually left. Goodall didn't even notice. He played until dawn.

Goodall represents an extreme. Yet it is easy to become engrossed in our own interests and needs. We can become too busy expressing ourselves to be aware of other people's needs.

Learn to listen not only with your ears but also with your mind and your heart. And be willing to let others play out their lives the best way they can.

Sacrifice and offering You do not desire, but You have given me an open ear. (Psalm 40:6)

Make it possible, Jesus, for us to be fully present to each other, to give each other undivided attention.

Taking the Long View

Oscar Romero, Archbishop of San Salvador, is hailed as a champion of the oppressed Salvadoran people. In fact, his opposition to injustice led to his assassination in 1980.

He understood the need – and the difficulty – of working for the future. But Archbishop Romero believed this: "It helps, now and then, to step back and take the long view. . . . We accomplish in our lifetime only a tiny fraction of the magnificent enterprise that is the Lord's work.

"We plant the seeds that will one day grow, we water the seeds already planted knowing they hold future promise. . . . We cannot do everything and there is a sense of liberation in realizing that. This enables us to do something, and to do it very, very well. It may be incomplete, but it is a beginning, a step along the way, an opportunity for the Lord's grace to enter and do the rest."

The Archbishop left a legacy of hope that the Salvadoran people will not forget.

What legacy will you leave?

A generation goes, and a generation comes, but the earth remains forever. (Ecclesiastes 1:4)

Sometimes I need to be reminded that I may never see the end results of my efforts. Holy God, You are the Master Builder. I am Your worker, to labor as You ask.

Notes from One Heart
to Another

Most of us are delighted to receive notes and letters. Yet we don't take the time or the trouble to write them as often as we could.

If that's your problem, consider what one Wisconsin man said about the notes he gets from his wife whenever he brown-bags his lunch. "I value them so much, I dump out whatever's edible to get to the note. I can tell her moods by her handwriting, and by what she says.

"What she doesn't know is that I've saved all her notes in a big shoe box. I'm afraid it would make her self-conscious to know how much I treasure them. Occasionally, I pull the box out, and leaf through them. It makes me feel good all over again."

Wife or husband, parent or child, friend or neighbor — you have something to say that someone would love to hear. Jot it down. Pass it along. And brighten someone else's day — and your own.

If one is mean to himself, to whom will he be generous? . . . No one is worse than one who is grudging to himself; this is the punishment for his meanness. (Sirach 14:5–6)

Teach me, Jesus, that graciousness to others begins with graciousness to myself and those closest to me.

Twain on Respect

Mark Twain had some memorable things to say about reverence, respect and faith: "Reverence for one's own sacred things . . . and respect for one's own beliefs — these are feelings which we cannot even help. They . . . are involuntary, like breathing . . .

"But the reverence which is difficult, and which has personal merit in it, is the respect which you pay, without compulsion to the political or religious attitude of a man whose beliefs are not yours."

Disagreements over religious or political matters too often become pointless exchanges of insults and put-downs.

Even though we disagree with another person's views, we can listen courteously and try to understand them. We can show the same respect that we would want others to have for our own beliefs.

Have unity of spirit, sympathy, love for one another, a tender heart, and a humble mind. (I Peter 3:8)

Holy Spirit, enable me to respect others, especially those very different from me.

Attitude and Abilities

Because of changing laws and attitudes, companies are beginning to do more for disabled employees than just provide for their physical needs and paying them a salary.

Wheelchair ramps and special telephones for the deaf are obviously important. But making disabled persons emotionally comfortable is important, too.

Some companies teach all employees to use the term "condition" rather than "defect," "disability" instead of "handicap," and "has" instead of "is afflicted with" or "is crippled by."

When we use language that reflects a positive, accepting attitude we show respect not only for the other person, but for ourselves as well.

It is not a question of being "politically correct." If we are kind, intelligent men and women who love our neighbors as we love ourselves, we are simply doing what we know is right.

Remember mercy. (Habakkuk 3:2)

May our tongues speak with heartfelt mercy, Spirit of Wisdom

A Springtime Harmony

The flowering of the woods in spring may seem haphazard, with each plant just doing its own thing. But botanists tell us the process is as carefully orchestrated as a symphony.

Flowers appear first on the small plants near the ground. These always bloom early, before the taller plants above them put out flowers and leaves – and shut out the sun.

Then in orderly succession, buds next unfurl on the shrubs, then the low trees, and finally the tallest trees – timed in perfect harmony.

We, too, need to be governed by harmony with ourselves, with others, and with God. Health, happiness, and spirituality are interrelated. Let us seek to live in the harmony that God offers us all.

Agree with God, and be at peace; in this way good will come to you. (Job 22:21)

Prince of Peace, how can I be at peace with my own self, others, You?

Rekindling Light and Warmth

You may have seen the sort of trick birthday candles that re-light when they are blown out. These novelty candles have wicks treated with magnesium crystals. The wicks retain heat so well that they rekindle themselves as soon as they are blown out.

These unquenchable little candles bring to mind the joy that comes from trusting God.

It's a joy that can't be extinguished by our circumstances. When others wrong us, we forgive them because we know that we, too, do wrong and need forgiveness. In times of trouble, or illness, or the death of a loved one, we don't despair, for we know that God is with us.

A joyful heart retains the warmth of God's love and is perpetually rekindled by it.

My times are in Your hand; deliver me . . . save me in Your steadfast love. (Psalm 31:15–16)

Father, I put my life in Your hands.

Being Kind

Kindness. It's usually so simple, so quiet a virtue that it can even pass unrecognized. Yet it makes the moment more pleasant for both giver and receiver. It is the civilizing touch that takes the brutish rush out of everyday living.

Our kindness to each other is also a reminder of God's kindness to us. God did not have to give us His Son, but in His great, overwhelming kindness, He did.

This little rhyme by an unknown author says it all:

Kindness is a little thing dropped in the heart's deep well.
The good, the joy that it may bring, time alone can tell.

Consider saying those few words to yourself frequently. They can serve as a reminder of kindness' importance in daily life.

Since I have dealt kindly with you, swear . . . that you in turn will deal kindly with my family. (Joshua 2:12)

Yes, Jesus, may we deal kindly with one another and with ourselves.

All Wrung Out

We all have days when we feel as if we've been put through the wringer. Scientists tell us that physically, that's what happens to us every day.

The spongy discs between the vertebrae of the spine are filled with liquid. During our waking hours, this fluid is gradually squeezed out. Then when we sleep, it's replaced.

Because of this loss of fluid, we may be as much as a third of an inch shorter at the end of the day than we are in the morning.

Emotionally, too, stressful situations can leave us drained. That's why we need some time for rest and relaxation to restore our emotional health.

We also need time for meditation and prayer for our spiritual well-being.

The prayer of the humble pierces the clouds, and it will not . . . desist until the Most High responds. (Sirach 35:21)

Holy Spirit, teach me how to care for my spiritual well-being.

Humor, Happiness and Health

Ready to laugh at some old and odd laws from around the country? These all concern behavior in church.

In Wheeler, Missouri, young girls are never allowed to walk a tightrope – unless it's in church.

In Leecreek, Arkansas, no one is allowed to attend church in any red-colored garment.

Turtle races are not permitted within one hundred yards of a local church at any time in Slaughter, Louisiana.

And in Blackwater, Kentucky, tickling a woman under her chin with a feather duster while in church carries a penalty of $10 and one day in jail.

Did these silly laws make you laugh? At least smile? That's great! A sense of humor is a key ingredient for a happy, healthy life.

When the Lord restored the fortunes of Zion, we were like those who dream. Our mouth was filled with laughter, and our tongue with shouts of joy. (Psalm 126:1–2)

Deliver me, Savior, from joylessness in every aspect of my life.

Cold Taste of Criticism

There's a good reason not to chill red wines.

In making white wine, the skins are removed before the grapes are fermented. But in making red wine the grapes are fermented with the skins on them. As a result, red wine contains several natural acids, such as tannic acid, not found in white wine.

Chilling a red wine masks the fruity flavor and brings out the harsh taste of the acids from the grape skins.

Unkind words might be compared to chilled red wine. Criticism made coldly and with indifference to another's feelings is acerbic and hurtful. The same criticism made in a warm, kindly way can be welcome and helpful.

Kindness always brings out the best in people.

The Lord's servant must not be quarrelsome but kindly to everyone. (2 Timothy 2:24)

God, forgive me my unkindnesses.

Vest Pocket Beauty

One April morning, New Yorkers passing a vest-pocket park were stopped by its beauty.

Two cherry trees were in full bloom. The wind was sending their pink petals swirling through the air like pink snow, covering the walks. In the background, a waterfall sparkled in the sun.

Many workers on their way to offices paused to enjoy the sight.

But not the park attendant. Armed with broom and dustpan, he was frantically trying to sweep up petals as they floated down. The expression on his face made it clear that he saw the delicate beauty only as litter that would have to be swept up and tossed out with the trash. He completely missed the fleeting, fragile moment of beauty the petals provided.

Undue concern about getting on with the tasks we have lined up in front of us can often blind us to the beauty in front of us right now.

Yes. We all have obligations. But we also have moments. They are just as real and just as important.

**Today's trouble is enough for today.
(Matthew 6:34)**

Help me enjoy the present rather than worry about the next hour, day, week, month or year, Lord, to whom belongs all time and all the seasons.

Reaching Out Long Distance

It is possible to nurture long distance friendships and family ties.

- Phone regularly, even if only to listen.
- Write, including news items, recipes, photos, anything the person would like to receive.
- Remember special days.
- Keep a list of important dates and personal preferences to help you select cards and gifts.
- Congratulate family and friends on their achievements.
- Provide support when they're having difficulties.
- Exchange visits with each other. But give plenty of notice in advance.

Maintaining close relationships with relatives and friends isn't easy, but, it is worth the effort. Having people we can count on and who can count on us — what could be more human?

I bow my knees before the Father, from whom every family in heaven and on earth takes its name. (Ephesians 3:14–15)

Heavenly Father, bless relatives and friends with respect for themselves and for each other.

Fly Balls at Fenway

Boston Red Sox fan Paul Lagace could not understand why the players no longer hit fly balls at Fenway Park the way they used to.

Lagace, a professor of aeronautics and astronautics, had students build a model of the ball park. Then they simulated the wind and typical paths of fly balls.

They found that the new club building behind home plate creates a vortex. The wind now swirls toward center field and back toward home plate. This pushes balls downward and backward with enough force to shorten fly balls by eight to twelve feet.

Our words, too, exert force. Belittling remarks can hurt and hinder those around us. Our own words can even hurt and hinder us. Encouraging words strengthen and help others as well as ourselves.

Be quick to listen, slow to speak, slow to anger. (James 1:19)

Encourage me to use Your gift of speech in love, Creator.

Symbols of Faith

You probably know that it is common for religious art to use symbols. Here's how Islamic art uses specific symbols to describe Paradise.

Blue lines represent water and the well-watered garden of Paradise; other lines, the rivers of milk, honey and wine flowing through the garden. An elaborate border represents the protective wall around Paradise; stylized trees, shrubs, fruits, indicate the lush and fruitful Islamic Paradise.

There is careful balance to the placement of each symbol. That's to remind the viewer that Paradise is an ordered place of rest.

Symbols used in all religious art represent deeper truths of faith. They are worth learning and enjoying. Art can be a wonderful introduction to spiritual traditions – your own and those of other people of faith. Visit a museum, pick up a book, visit a house of worship. Enrich yourself.

In the beginning, God created the heavens and the earth. (Genesis 1:1)

God of all, I do have faith. Strengthen it, mend it, tend it, nurture it.

Toad Tales

Often we judge other people, even other creatures, by appearance.

Consider the toad. This little warty, rough-skinned, nocturnal garden dweller with bulging eyes, short, fat legs, and dull brownish coloring will never win a beauty contest. And the poisonous liquid its skin secretes when threatened makes it unappetizing to other animals.

But its wonderfully long, sticky tongue with its snap-out-roll-back motion efficiently delivers garden pest meals to the toad, making it a gardener's ally.

Instead of judging by appearances, or even by usefulness (as with the ugly but useful toad) look for the true value within others.

It's no fairy tale to say you just might find more princes and princesses than you could have guessed.

The measure you give will be the measure you get back. (Luke 6:38)

Open my eyes to see the inner beauty of every person, every creature, Creator who delights in variety.

Great Expectations for Yourself

Eugene Ormandy was one of the great orchestra leaders in American history. He led the Philadelphia Orchestra for forty-four years after the renowned Leopold Stokowski.

Yet Eugene Ormandy was a disappointment to his father. The elder Ormandy wanted his son to become a famous violinist.

His father's expectations troubled him, but did not deter Eugene Ormandy from his dream of becoming a conductor. He was always true to his own values. One critic said of him, "He never gave a bad performance."

If you choose your values carefully, and set high standards for yourself, you will not have to worry about others' expectations.

William Shakespeare wrote: "To thine own self be true, and . . . thou canst not then be false to any man." That famous quote is worth remembering when you are tempted to give up what really matters to you.

You are of more value than many sparrows. (Luke 12:7)

When I am down, Lord, convince me of my infinite worth in Your sight.

Baskets of Blessings

Lent is a perfect time to combine spiritual concerns with practical matters.

Bernie Glade knows that holiday traditions mean a great deal to youngsters, but that families in need are sometimes forgotten. So the Port Byron, Illinois, woman decided to help.

"Each year I make Easter baskets to give to some elementary school students (and their younger siblings) whose families would have to struggle to provide holiday treats. A woman's group and Sunday school classes at my church contribute useful items as well as fun ones, school supplies, socks, hair ribbons, books, small toys and wrapped candies," she says.

"My junior high Sunday school class helps assemble the baskets. The finished baskets are then given to the school nurse to distribute in order to protect the privacy of the families."

Instead of simply giving up something for Lent, why not actually give something?

I have indeed received much joy and encouragement from Your love. (Philemon 7)

Let Easter joy shine in us and through us for all Your dear children, whatever their ages, Christ Jesus.

Delightful, Imperfect Creation

A group of history buffs dedicated a plaque to two stray dogs that died well over a hundred years ago.

These two dogs, named Lameth and Bummer, were such devoted friends that they captured the hearts of San Francisco citizens. When Bummer died, Mark Twain wrote his obituary, saying that Bummer died "full of years and honor and disease and fleas."

The humorist's wry observation about the canine condition reminds us of the human condition as well. Even the most beloved and saintly among us have our flaws and weaknesses. That's something we forget when we condemn ourselves for falling short of perfection.

God wants us to be our best selves, but He doesn't hate us for our imperfections. God loves and delights in us, always and unconditionally.

Clear me from hidden faults. (Psalm 19:12)

Loving Redeemer, save me from myself, my pride, my determination to "go it alone" without You.

Nothing Trifling about Truffles

Father Pierre Gleize is delighted when parishioners drop fungus into the collection plate. His parish is in southern France, and the fungus given as an offering is truffles. This gourmet delicacy commands such a high price that it's called the "black diamond." The offerings of truffles are sold to support the church.

In a homily, Father Gleize told churchgoers in this truffle-producing area, "Christians should embellish the world the way truffles embellish a meal. Love transforms everything. Isn't that just what a good truffle does to an omelet, paté or poultry dish?"

One person's loving goodwill can add a special joy to the lives of others. Love does transform everything.

Jesus answered him, "Those who love Me will keep My word, and My Father will love them, and We will come to them and make Our home with them." (John 14:23)

Redeemer, may our love for You find its expression in loving service.

A Haven of Welcome

Young Alan Marshall of Windham, Connecticut, suffered a serious head injury a few years ago and had to spend a lot of time at a Boston rehabilitation center.

They could have been hard days for the boy and his parents. Luckily, the Markert family and the Hospitality Program helped. Angie and Tom Markert are among the volunteer hosts who open their homes to folks like the Marshalls, families of patients who must travel for medical treatment. They find friendly — and free — lodgings through networks of hospitality groups.

Hosts need to be sensitive since some guests like companionship and others do not. They also have to realize that not all situations end happily. Still, the main criterion, according to Tom Markert, is "the desire to help people."

That's a desire that ought to be appreciated and cultivated. Give yourself — and others — a pat on the back when you help out a neighbor — or a stranger.

God gives the desolate a home to live in.
(Psalm 68:6)

Jesus, You and Mary and Joseph knew what it was like to travel without knowing if you would have a haven at the end of the day. Remind me to welcome those in need.

Disarming Weapons and Hostility

When the U.S. Navy was testing a new torpedo back in 1962, it encountered a strange problem. Whenever the sonar device sent out a targeting sound, it would be answered from under water. These mysterious answers caused the torpedo to go off course.

For two years the Navy tried to find the source of the interference. Finally, they discovered that the sounds came from dolphins trying to make friends with the torpedo. Friendliness was literally making a weapon ineffective.

Friendliness can often be disarming in a different way, turning aside anger and hostility. These feelings often grow out of hurt or fear, and friendliness can soothe and reassure. Even if your first reaction to unkindness is retaliation, try something better. You just might gain a friend.

A soft answer turns away wrath, but a harsh word stirs up anger. (Proverbs 15:1)

Who needs to be disarmed by my friendly, patient words, Savior?

Rich Beginnings

In his book *You Don't Have to Be in Who's Who to Know What's What*, humorist Sam Levenson said this about his childhood:

"Speaking for myself, and perhaps for some other alumni of the slums, I must declare that I was not a poor child; I just didn't have any money."

He went on to describe a loving and supportive family which had high ideals and cared deeply about others.

A recent study confirms that what is most important to a child's future success and happiness is not economic status, but warm, loving parents.

Each child deserves such riches. Endow every child in your life with the treasure of your love. It's the legacy of a lifetime.

Let us love, not in word or speech, but in truth and action. (1 John 3:18)

Loving Lord, enable parents to love their children generously, sincerely and impartially.

The First Tax Shelter?

When we see newspaper headlines about a millionaire engaging in tax fraud, we tend to associate this form of dishonesty with modern manipulations, but it seems to be an ancient form of cheating.

Second-century biographer and historian Gaius Suetonius Tranquillis wrote about tax evasion by the celebrated Roman poet Virgil two centuries earlier. Virgil held a funeral for a dead fly, complete with pallbearers and eulogies, then buried the fly on land surrounding his villa. In ancient Rome, land used for cemeteries was not taxable, so Virgil made his property technically a burial ground – and tax exempt.

The rich and famous do not have a monopoly on tax cheating. It seems to be a form of dishonesty many otherwise scrupulous people engage in. Someone who upon finding a wallet immediately contacts the owner, or who rushes back to a store to return an extra $5 mistakenly given in change, too often turns around and claims phony deductions on his or her income tax returns.

It's not really possible to have two standards of integrity – one for our daily life and another for April 15th. The government being cheated is not some vague abstraction: it's the people of our nation . . . we ourselves.

The commandments . . . "You shall not steal; You shall not covet" . . . are summed up in this word, "Love your neighbor as yourself." (Romans 13:9)

Help me be honest and just, Jesus.

Images of Our Loving God

The Scriptures use beautiful, poetic images to describe the relationship between God and His people.

Delighting in God's commandments, we are said to be like drought-resistant evergreens beside flowing water.

Or like green olive trees planted in God's house, still vigorous in old age.

Again, we are described as fledgling eaglets learning to fly.

Jesus said we were His little flock of sparrows.

Or we are thirsty deer yearning for life-giving water.

And Haggai the prophet said we were like a signet ring on God's fingers so much does God love us.

These vivid, touching words clearly show the depth and closeness of our relationship with God. What images, what words would you use? Use them the next time you pray.

"How often have I desired to gather your children together as a hen gathers her brood under her wings, and you were not willing!" (Luke 13:34)

Loving Lord, take me like Your chick under Your wing.

Secret of a Job Done Well

An elderly woman on a fixed income took in ironing. And there was always a great demand for her work. Compliments abounded. Her customers raved about the way their shirts looked.

Ironing a shirt is ironing a shirt you say. Yes, but, she had a secret.

As she dampened each shirt she thought about the wearer. She pictured the good that would happen to him. Finally she offered the benefit of her prayers and of the work of ironing itself for the shirt's wearer.

Her secret was loving prayer.

Whatever your trade or profession, make room for love and prayer. Remember those touched by your work. Ask for God's help in giving your best to every individual you affect through your job. Turn over your work to God. You just might find your own secret to a job well done.

Live your life in a manner worthy of the gospel of Christ. (Philippians 1:27)

Bless those who work for me, Lord.

One Neighborly Church

The members of a church outreach committee in Auburn, California, wanted to help their community. They found a girls' group home where the residents needed interested adults to show them that they were valuable to others and to God. The girls had all been neglected and abused. They didn't believe anyone cared about them.

So the church, St. Luke's Episcopal, developed a life skills program for the young women. They learned how to cook, sew, perform first aid and CPR. They were also treated to manicures and haircuts.

The effort of the church and their neighbors who volunteered their time and talents showed the girls that someone cared.

Does your church have a similar program? If so, why not help out. If not, why not start one? There are young people who could benefit from any attention you can share with them.

"Just as I have loved you, you also should love one another. By this everyone will know that you are My disciples." (John 13:34–35)

Jesus, enable me to overcome any aversion to getting involved.

Use All You've Got

After the bombing of the Alfred P. Murrah building in Oklahoma City in 1995, people from all over the country came to help. Susan Close was one of them.

Close is a native of nearby Moore, Oklahoma. She drove to the site of the bombing daily, and delivered clean clothes and laundry to the volunteer workers. She did it even though she uses a wheelchair.

"I told them just because I'm handicapped doesn't mean I can't do something," Close said.

How often do we say, "I'm only one person. I can't change the world?"

Look at the big picture. Realize that the world is made up of individuals – young, old, able-bodied, disabled, men, women – who, together, can make a huge difference in the way things are.

No one else can do the job God has entrusted to you.

This is love, that we walk according to His commandments. (2 John 6)

Don't let me make excuses for being less than my best, loving Savior.

An Apple for the Stranger

Life in the big city has its ups and downs. For Frank Sweeney, falling down on the streets of New York had a definite up-side to it.

Leaving a greengrocer with a shopping bag filled with apples, he tripped on a broken curb and fell into the intersection, surrounded by the apples which had tumbled from his bag.

In the time it took him to get up and dust himself off, the apples – all thirty of them – were once again resting in their sack, thanks to the quick work of half a dozen people.

The incident left the apple-buyer and his fruit barely bruised. Indeed, the New Yorker was happily surprised by the courtesy of the men and women who took a few seconds out of their day to perform a small but appreciated kindness for a stranger.

Every new day dawns with the opportunity to show respect for God through respect for neighbor. Your opportunity might be as small as an apple, but your response will be as big as your heart.

A word fitly spoken is like apples of gold in a setting of silver. (Proverbs 25:11)

In all the little ways, but especially by being kind, may I indeed love my neighbor as I love myself, Jesus.

Easing Grief

Do you remember St. John's account of the Crucifixion? John was the disciple whom Jesus loved – some say His best friend.

John and Mary the mother of Jesus stayed at the foot of Jesus' cross. Just before he died, Jesus looked at his mother and said, "Woman, behold your son." And to John, He said, "Behold your mother."

Why did Jesus do this?

He knew that His mother and His friend would be grief-stricken at His death. So He gave them each other, knowing that each could ease the other's grief. They would be there for one another, caring for and looking after one another.

When you ease the grief of another person, you follow the example of Jesus – you become Christ-like. Be there for those who are grieving. They need you.

[Jesus] had compassion for her. (Luke 7:13)

Compassionate Jesus, may I treat others with that compassion with which You've treated me.

Between Youngsters and God

Children talk to God quite naturally. And parents should encourage them.

"The home is the most fertile ground for our inner growth," says psychologist Edward Hoffman. "There each child has the opportunity to gain a strong moral awareness, an appreciation for life and a sense of God's presence in the daily world."

How can parents nurture this budding spirituality? First, use a child's own questions and interests to relate everyday events to our Creator and emphasize virtues such as charity, justice and courage.

Second, pray with your child.

And thirdly, while it may be a truism, actions do speak louder than words. So if you live the kind of meaningful, spiritually rich life you want your youngsters to emulate, they probably will.

See the world through a child's eyes and you may gain a clearer vision.

"Receive the kingdom of God as a little child." (Mark 10:15)

Father, restore my sense of wonder and clear vision.

Alone with God

When reading the Bible, we sometimes forget that it is more than just a literary masterpiece. It is God's Word.

Sometimes it is easy to find comfort and inspiration in one passage or another. At other times, for whatever reason, it is almost impossible.

One way to meditate on God's Word is to just sit quietly and imagine a particular scene. Take for example, the night Jesus spent in Gethsemane. Imagine Him praying, "let this cup pass from Me; yet not what I want but what You want" (Matthew 26:39). Does Jesus whisper or shout? Is the air hot and dry, or humid? What sorts of trees, bushes, flowers are there? How does it feel to overhear Jesus?

Or imagine the night Jesus calmed the storm (Matthew 8:24–26). Can you feel the fear of the fishermen in the boat? How would you describe the waves? Let Jesus speak. How do His words affect you?

Try this technique with other scripture passages. Remember that Jesus and the other people in the Bible did live, walk, talk, eat and sleep in a particular country at a particular time. Open up the Bible, and refresh yourself.

All scripture is inspired by God and is useful for teaching, for reproof, for correction, and for training in righteousness. (2 Timothy 3:16–17)

Word of God, open my mind to understand the Scriptures.

Danger at Home

A nine-year-old boy was playing when he found a gun, loaded it with ammunition, leaned out a window and fired. The bullet just missed someone in a neighboring office building and lodged in a wall.

The child then unloaded the gun but continued to look out the window. That's how the police found him with twenty unspent bullets. A family friend had left the gun and bullets in the apartment.

Questioned, the boy said he had learned how to load the gun by watching television.

That raises two points for parents. Pay attention to your children's TV viewing. Think carefully before you allow a gun in your home for any reason.

Teach your children that violence solves nothing. Make your home a place of peace.

The land is full of bloody crimes and the city is full of violence. (Ezekiel 7:23)

Prince of Peace, show us how to renounce crime and violence.

Believing in a Fiddler

Violin teacher Dorothy DeLay's students consider her the best teacher in the world. She's also their counselor and friend.

Probably the most famous of her former students is Itzhak Perlman. But DeLay did more than teach violin to the young Perlman. She helped build his self-confidence after polio had left him with serious disabilities.

Thirty years later, Perlman said of her, "She believed in me. There was a time when my parents and Miss DeLay were the only people in the world who believed I could have a career. The fact that I was disabled . . . people looked at me with distorted vision. And she never did. She was able to see."

To see and bring out the best in others is one of the most precious gifts one person can ever give another. Open your eyes – and praise the good you see around you.

Bear one another's burdens. (Galatians 6:2)

Giver of every talent and ability, help teachers and parents to encourage young people's gifts.

Salute to Fair Play

It's great to hear about the victories of athletes, but what about athletes who consider fair play more important than winning?

The British kayak team lost the world championship race in 1990. But what caused them to lose the race won them the Pierre de Coubertin International Fair Play Trophy.

The British team was in second place in the race, with the Danish team leading. Then the Danish team's rudder was damaged and the British team stopped to help them fix it.

The race continued, and the Danes beat the British by one second! If the British had taken advantage of the other team's accident, they would have won. But they valued fair play more than winning.

The real winners, in life as in sports, are those who show nobility of spirit.

Do you not know that in a race the runners all compete, but only one receives the prize? Run in such a way that you may win it. (I Corinthians 9:24)

Courteous Lord, give me a share of Your courtesy even as You give me the ability to run the race and receive the prize — life eternal.

The Taste of Togetherness

The disappearing dining room is one sign of change in modern life.

Just a few decades ago, the whole family gathered at the dining table for meals and conversation. Today, many homes don't even have a dining room.

Not that it matters where a family eat their meals. What does matter is that many families rarely have a meal together at all. Fathers, mothers and teenagers work. Adults and young people participate in a variety of activities, rarely together. Folks eat on the run, so meals are often take-outs or frozen dinners heated in the microwave. It's not unusual for each family member to prepare his or her own meal.

Something valuable is being lost. Maybe busy families can't share every meal, but they need some time together. It's important for families to discuss their everyday news as well as major events. They need to share their ideas and feelings.

Think about it. Talk about it. Make time for each other.

Whoever does not provide for relatives, and especially for family members, has denied the faith. (1 Timothy 5:8)

Thanks for all the members of my family, God, when they are easy to love and when they aren't.

Turning a Parish into a Farm

St. Joseph's, an Apple Creek, Missouri, church decided that they could share their forty park-like acres with seventeen rabbits and a dozen chickens. That, they reasoned, would provide homegrown protein for the poor.

Then a parish council member who worked with "Operation St. Isidore," a local church effort to supply fresh food to the needy, suggested that there was room to actually supply beef to those who could rarely afford it.

Two eight-month-old Black Angus steers, prime beef on the hoof, arrived shortly afterwards.

Parishioners took a while getting used to the glossy black beauties on their church's emerald lawn. But they knew they were helping to feed the hungry.

Is there something you can do to help feed the hungry? What about your church? A club or group you belong to? There are things you can do on your own. But, sometimes, working with others can produce prime results.

Share your bread with the hungry. (Isaiah 58:7)

Jesus, who did bless the loaves and fishes, show us how to share the bread of our lives with those hungry for food and more than food.

Technological Advances in Communication

"To communicate" is a verb meaning to make known, to convey knowledge or information, to transmit thoughts or feelings.

Supposedly, communication — the act and art of transmitting knowledge, information, thoughts or feelings — is improving hourly, if not minute-by-minute, through technology.

We have phones and faxes, modems and computers, e-mail and answering machines. Let's not forget old-fashioned letters, memos and notes.

If worse comes to worst we can talk face to face.

But is communication improving? Not according to the words of one cartoon: "What do you mean we don't communicate? Just yesterday I faxed you a reply to the recorded message you left me on my answering machine!"

Is your communication improving? Or in need of improvement?

Give ear, O My people, to My teaching; incline your ears to the words of My mouth. (Psalm 78:1)

May we remember that good communication involves listening as well as speaking, Holy Spirit.

Colors in a Rainbow

Rainbows are created whenever it rains, but to see them you have to be in the right position in relation to the sun.

And what you see is yours alone. Ten people who seem to be looking at the same rainbow are actually seeing *ten different* rainbows because no two people look at a rainbow from exactly the same angle.

When sunlight strikes drops of rain, the light is bent and separated into its constituent colors. Each raindrop contains all the colors, but contributes just one color at a time to a rainbow. As each raindrop falls and its angle to your eyes changes, its color changes. And the different colors come out at different angles, producing a multi-colored band.

People are as individual as the rainbows they see.

Each person in his or her own way adds beauty to the world. Each person has special qualities that can make the world a better place. Our gifts take many forms. And each quality is a talent for being, living and doing in a unique way.

Each of us was given grace according to the measure of Christ's gift . . . to equip the saints for the work of . . . building up the body of Christ. (Ephesians 4:7–12)

That I might discover and appreciate the gifts You've given me, Holy Spirit!

Portrait of One Busy Woman

Until recently in history most women married, raised families, kept house and never developed personal careers. Then there were the exceptions.

Sofonisba Anguissola, a sixteenth century Italian noblewoman, is among those who have proved it is possible to do everything expected of women and still have a flourishing career.

One of six sisters to be given advanced education in the arts, music and letters, Anguissola was later apprenticed to an artist. Study with the great Michelangelo followed; then appointment as a court painter; and later marriage and a large family.

In her nineties Anguissola was not only still painting but also teaching others, among them Van Dyck.

Whatever decisions you make about how to live your life, give it your all.

A capable wife . . . considers a field and buys it . . . plants a vineyard . . . opens her hand to the poor . . . makes linen garments and sells them . . . opens her mouth with wisdom and the teaching of kindness. (Proverbs 31:10, 16, 20, 24, 26)

Jesus, Son of Mary, bless women and men in balancing their lives and giving the best they have.

Beauty Found in Flaws

Do you tend to measure yourself against others and think of your differences as imperfections?

Next time you're belittling yourself, remember what gives emeralds their beautiful color: a trace of an element that also makes them flawed.

Emeralds are a form of the common mineral beryl. What makes emeralds different is that they contain a small amount of chromium. The chromium atoms replace some of the aluminum atoms found in beryl crystals. Since the chromium atoms are larger, they squeeze the crystal structure, cracking it. But they also give the emerald its distinctive color and make it immensely valuable.

The small traits that make us uniquely different also give us our individuality – special qualities that can add beauty to the world.

Have no fear, My servant Jacob, says the Lord, and do not be dismayed, O Israel; for I am going to save you from far away, and your offspring from the land of their captivity . . . And you shall be My people, and I will be your God. (Jeremiah 30:10, 22)

Creator who delights in diversity, help me delight in my own uniqueness and that of my fellow human beings.

Nine-Letter Word
for Compulsion

Years ago, a woman complained in a Chicago court that her husband spent so much time doing crossword puzzles that he wasn't providing for his family. The court decreed that the husband must limit himself to three crossword puzzles a day!

Drug and alcohol abuse aren't the only harmful addictions. Many other types of compulsive behavior can destroy a family or a life. Gambling, eating, even doing crossword puzzles can be destructive if they get out of control and dominate our lives.

If some addiction is threatening the well-being of you or your family, take steps to free yourself. Seek help from a counselor or support group to get it under control. Change is hard, but it is possible.

With God's grace there is always hope.

The Spirit of the Lord . . . has sent me to proclaim release to the captives. (Luke 4:18)

Does some aspect of my life need liberation from an addiction, Divine Liberator?

Helping Others, Helping Himself

Paul Adams has found that helping other people also helps him. As part of his treatment for mental illness, Adams does volunteer work assisting elderly people — going on errands, escorting them to doctor's offices, and so on.

"Before I started doing this," says Adams, "I would lie in bed and be depressed all day. Volunteering gets my mind off my own burdens and makes me responsible."

He's an accomplished pianist and performs at senior citizens' centers. As he entertains others, he benefits, too. He says he has learned to deal with the pressure of performing in public.

Many people find that when they help others, they receive as much as they give. Their own lives become more meaningful and fulfilling.

Those who are generous are blessed.
(Proverbs 22:9)

Enable me to help the depressed and the down-hearted, Lord.

One Perfect Day

If you could, wouldn't you delight in living just one day doing God's will with your whole heart, being exactly the person God created you to be?

Most of us would say yes.

And at the end of that special day we'd praise and bless God with special fervor and sincerity.

The Mozarabic Liturgy, used in Spain from the ninth to fifteenth centuries, has a lovely prayer asking for God's help in trying to live up to that ideal.

"Grant us, O Lord, to pass this day in gladness and in peace without stumbling and without stain, that reaching the eventide victorious over all temptation, we may praise You, the eternal God, Who is blessed, and Who governs all things."

Praise the Lord, for the Lord is good; sing to His name, for He is gracious. (Psalm 135:3)

Lord, keep me from temptation and guide my feet on Your way of peace.

Fair Words Work

Felix Mendelssohn, one of the most popular composers of his day, was generous in recognizing and promoting the work of others.

Once, at a gathering in London, a group of opera buffs were ripping to shreds Donizetti's opera *The Daughter of the Regiment.* Among the detractors were composers who couldn't hold a candle to Donizetti.

Mendelssohn listened to their comments. Then he said, "Well, I don't know. I'm afraid I like it. I should like to have written it myself."

So, obviously, would the envious folks belittling the opera. Their snide remarks stopped. The good-natured fairness of one person silenced a roomful of spiteful critics.

It's a technique that works. Try it for yourself.

Do not judge by appearances, but judge with right judgment. (John 7:24)

May a non judgmental attitude and good-natured fairness be qualities of my character, Lord.

Hope to Keep Going

Webster's defines hope as a longing with the "expectation or belief in fulfillment."

In his letter to the Romans, St. Paul said that "if we hope for what we do not see, we wait for it with patience."

Patience is part of hope, but as the founder of The Christophers, Rev. James Keller, M.M., wrote:

> Hope looks for the good in people, instead of
>   harping on the worst.
> Hope discovers what can be done, instead of
>   grumbling about what cannot.
> Hope pushes ahead when it might be easy to quit.
> Hope opens doors where despair closes them.
> Hope accepts tragedy with courage.

Hope therefore is not just a longing, it is an active working toward the improvement of our world.

Hoping against hope, [Abraham] believed that he would become "the father of many nations."
(Romans 4:18)

God of my ancestors Abraham and Sarah, give me that hope with which they were blessed.

Brighten Your Life

Ever feel life has a dull sameness to it? You can brighten your day. Here are some tips for enriching your life and the many lives you touch:

- Focus on the present, the future. Learn from the past. Don't dwell on it.
- Look for ways, both simple and more demanding, to spread kindness.
- Use your energy to solve problems, not to run away or fight circumstances.
- Have fun: play a game; tell a joke; sing a song; take a walk; enjoy a hobby.
- Believe in something bigger than your self. God wants you to have ideals, goals.
- Pray. Enjoy God's company. Beg for the desire and courage to do His will. Bring Him your needs and others'.

The Lord is my portion; I promise to keep Your words. I implore Your favor with all my heart. (Psalm 119:57–58)

That You are my portion and my way makes each moment lovely, God.

To Rise Like a Phoenix

Minneapolis social workers Chuck Beattie and Bret Byfield were angry about the lack of helpful services for homeless people. They knew that the key to getting folks off the streets was to find them jobs, a community and a sense of purpose.

Armed with a few private donations and much optimism, they bought run-down houses and hired homeless people to help fix them up. Then they moved those same people in so they would benefit from their own work.

The Phoenix Group now houses more than three hundred tenants, all of whom had been homeless. A supermarket, an art gallery and an auto body shop also employ the residents. One man who had been homeless and a drug addict now has a job and has regained his dignity and his family. "I don't make a lot of money, but I feel like I'm a king," he says. "Nothing can stop me."

Two men willing to put a good idea to work have made a difference for hundreds of others. Don't let doubts about your own abilities or chances for success stop you before you get started.

**Cursed be anyone who deprives the alien, the orphan, and the widow of justice.
(Deuteronomy 27:19)**

Help us give all our brothers and sisters that justice which is their right, God.

Sing a Song of Courage

The Great Day Chorale is an *a cappella* group that performs gospel music in its traditional form.

Louvinia Pointer, co-director of the Brooklyn group, feels that gospel music often becomes so showy that it loses much of its sincerity. That's why the Great Day Chorale sings spirituals as they might have been sung by slaves on plantations.

Ms. Pointer says, "The message of courage and determination that's all through the spirituals is a message that we need. They encouraged each other. They admonished each other. As far back as I can go, I can't find a spiritual that has any tinge of bitterness or hatred."

The Gospel message of hope gives us the strength to press on, even under the most burdensome circumstances.

The time is fulfilled, and the kingdom of God has come near, repent, and believe in the good news. (Mark 1:15)

Come, Word of God, and do not delay.

Responsible, Not Self-Righteous

Every single one of us has the responsibility of looking after our health and of respecting our own physical well-being and that of others. Smoking is dangerous. Drinking too much alcohol and caffeine as well as consuming excess sugar, fat, salt, and calories can hurt us.

But there are attitudes that can also cause harm.

Writer Antoinette Bosco objects to "beliefs that we can exert almost total control over our lives and that if anything interferes with our perceived control we have a right to dress down the interferer and make him feel small." That, she says, "is not a superior lifestyle. It is mean-spiritedness . . .[and] has no place in our world."

Indeed, there is no place for intolerance anywhere, especially when it is based on self-righteousness. There is a huge difference between trying to bring out the best in yourself and others and believing that you can, or should, control everything.

Do not reach out your hand for everything you see. (Sirach 31:14)

Enable me, Jesus, to practice moderation as I enjoy all the Father's good gifts.

A Helping Hand
– and Much More

Sometimes a small act of kindness is far bigger than we think.

Truck driver Will Maguire stopped to help a stranded motorist on a Maryland highway. He saw that the woman was very upset so he reassured her. Then he fixed the flat tire. When she offered to pay her rescuer, he graciously refused.

What Will Maguire didn't know was that the motorist had been raped several years before. Alone in her car, she felt overwhelmed with fear as the traffic roared past. Then a stranger gave her a helping hand.

"Even if he didn't see why what he had done made him great, to me he was a hero," the woman said later. "He stopped and cared and gave a damn."

Stopping and caring seems like a huge effort some days. But the good you do is not always clear to you. A little thing can mean the whole world to a someone in need of what you can give.

Blessed are the merciful, for they will receive mercy. (Matthew 5:7)

Show us who needs our merciful help, Lord.

Discovering Magic in Paper

When Lillian Oppenheimer's daughter was recovering from meningitis, her mother looked for a way to entertain her. She found it in origami.

Mrs. Oppenheimer's interest in the ancient Japanese art of paper-folding continued over the years. By the 1950's, her hobby had gained her a following. The popularity of creating beautiful pieces of art from sheets of special paper had spread across America.

Today, origami is used in art therapy classes because it offers a sense of accomplishment and satisfaction. From simple to complex, the forms range from fantasy dragons to birds in flight to geodesic balls.

Mrs. Oppenheimer learned an art form from another culture, and finding magic in a piece of paper, invited others to enjoy her hobby and find beauty.

Beauty is part of life. Seek it out to enjoy and to share.

Ah, you are beautiful, my love.
(Song of Solomon 1:15)

Yes, God, You are beautiful — You are Beauty itself!

Perfection No Requirement

The myth that mothers should be perfect or never "get mad" does a lot of harm.

Like everybody else, mothers become annoyed, resentful, angry. Some women think that having these feelings makes them failures as mothers. They're wrong.

A psychologist's job is to handle emotions. Yet a recent survey showed that ninety percent of clinical psychologists have felt anger toward at least one patient. For a therapist, experiencing the feeling is not a matter for concern. What's important is being able to handle the feeling appropriately.

The same is true for mothers. Having some negative feelings is not wrong. What matters is controlling them so they don't harm anyone, especially children.

Being a good mother means being human in its best sense. Not perfect.

Honor your father and your mother.
(Exodus 20:12)

Jesus, enable parents and their children to honor and respect each other.

"If I were You . . . "

The founder of the world-famous Mayo Clinic, Dr. Charles Mayo, made a valuable rule for himself. "When I am your doctor," he said, "I try to imagine the kind of doctor I'd like if I were you. Then I try to be that kind of doctor."

That's a good idea, whoever we are or whatever we do. It's easy to forget that we don't all think the same way or have exactly the same feelings about problems – or even about good things. There's a big difference between asking yourself "How would I feel in that situation?" and "How is that person feeling and how would I want to be treated if I felt that way?"

Staying sensitive to the needs of others sometimes demands a lot of us. But a thoughtful and generous spirit is worth cultivating.

Love is patient; love is kind; love is not envious or boastful or arrogant or rude. It does not insist on its own way; it is not irritable or resentful. (I Corinthians 13:4–5)

Make me a genuine lover, Loving Lord.

Finding Real Happiness

Most people would probably agree that they want to be happy. But defining what happiness is, what it means to us and how to grasp it, isn't easy at all.

Here are a couple of ideas that might stir your own thinking. "It is an illusion to think that more comfort means happiness," according to writer Storm Jameson. "Happiness comes of the capacity to feel deeply, to enjoy simply, to think freely, to risk life, to be needed."

And the author of many American classics, Nathaniel Hawthorne, believed that "happiness is a butterfly, which, when pursued, is always just beyond your grasp; but which, if you sit down quietly, may alight upon you."

However we describe it, happiness comes to us not by seeking it for its own sake, but by living lives of loving action.

Happy are those . . . [whose] delight is in the law of the Lord, and on His law they meditate day and night. (Psalm 1:1–2)

That You and Your law of love might indeed be my delight, Lord, my joy.

Saving Young and Old from Suicide

One of the tragedies of our time is the loneliness and isolation so many people feel. It is one of the facts behind the terrible statistic that a million people a year attempt suicide.

Relatively few succeed. Yet it is troubling that the suicide rate is highest among the aged and young teens.

Both groups represent our most important national resources. Older men and women represent collective knowledge and experience; the young, our future. Why should anyone of any age think that life is meaningless, hopeless?

There are no easy answers.

Anything that you do to convince a person of his or her worth will be a great blessing. It can not only save a life, but give that life real meaning.

God made human beings straightforward, but they have devised many schemes. (Ecclesiastes 7:29)

Remind us of our basic goodness, Lord who formed us from the clay of the earth.

Our Street, Our Responsibility

There was so much trash and broken glass along Springfield Street in Lawrence, Massachusetts, that Steven Clarke was afraid that his two young sons would cut their feet.

So he joined with two elderly neighbors and spent a long day filling barrels with debris and sweeping the sidewalks and streets. Both older men have health problems, but persisted in their task. One said, "Maybe people will think twice about throwing something down."

While nobody thought one cleanup would solve the problem permanently, neighbors were happy with the results and the efforts of the three volunteers.

Steven Clarke said all he wanted was a safe place for his children to play. "It's my block. It's my street," he said. That's a good reason for any of us.

Anyone, then, who knows the right thing to do and fails to do it, commits sin. (James 4:17)

How can I express my concern for my neighborhood, God?

Clearing Clutter

If you've been putting off clearing out the clutter in your home, here are some ideas from a time management expert.

Get some big cardboard boxes and label them:

- Trash – for those things of no use to you or anybody else.
- Charity – for items useful to others.
- Posterity – for sentimental items.
- Transition – for things that need to be sorted through carefully.

Then go to work, one room at a time, or even one drawer at a time.

Approaching any goal just one step at a time rather than worrying about doing everything completely and perfectly is a sound idea.

Add persistence to a well-thought-out plan and you may accomplish more than you thought possible.

Better is a little with the fear of the Lord than great treasure and trouble with it. (Proverbs 15:16)

Jesus, enable me to simplify my life, not just my home, so that reverence for You may be my chief treasure.

Teacher Discourages Coarse Language

A teacher in California who was tired of hearing her students swear and curse came up with a creative plan.

Deidre Harris, a teacher at Crenshaw High School, started fining her students each time they used a profanity in her classroom. The students expanded the idea to include other insults. The penalties ranged from five cents for each "shut up" to a quarter for the "f-word."

Harris saves the money to use for a party for the kids at the end of the semester. One year, she surprised them by having rap star Heavy D appear at the school. He was a role model because of his song, *Don't Curse.*

Treating offensive behavior with humor and creativity can sometimes solve the problem. Be sure to add good example for good measure.

Do not accustom your mouth to coarse, foul language for it involves sinful speech. (Sirach 23:13)

Inspire teachers to handle offensive behavior with humor, creativity and patience, Holy Spirit.

Speak Up for Understanding

A man learned firsthand how stereotypes are formed. He was often disturbed on the subway by Chinese people speaking loudly. At first he assumed they had a hearing impairment. But when it happened repeatedly, he began to think that many Chinese were rude.

Then he learned that these people were speaking Cantonese, and that it's a difficult language. The same word can often mean different things, depending upon the tone in which it's spoken. And Cantonese has more than twice as many tones as Mandarin, the other major Chinese language.

To make the slight difference in tone clear and make themselves understood most people speaking Cantonese develop the habit of speaking loudly.

That's why fellow commuters were speaking so loudly. As usual, ignorance breeds stereotypes while knowledge and understanding dispel them. Be willing to educate yourself and make an effort to gain insight.

Make every effort to supplement your faith with virtue, and virtue with knowledge. (2 Peter 1:5)

Lord, increase my faith and knowledge.

Sheba to the Rescue

Extraordinary mother love – human, finned, furred, feathered or scaled – stirs our admiration. Here's the story of Sheba and her nine newborn puppies.

Sheba's owner didn't want her puppies.

He leashed Sheba to a fence, then buried her nine puppies alive in a shallow sandy grave. Sheba strained at her leash for almost twenty-four hours before breaking free. Then she used her large, strong paws and claws – she's part Rottweiler – to rescue them.

She hurt her neck breaking free of the leash. But six of her very sandy and very hungry puppies survived.

When word got out, hundreds of people wanted to adopt one of the little survivors. Meanwhile Sheba enjoyed being with them and they with her.

Her owner faced animal abuse charges.

Animals deserve protection. Children need it even more. Show respect and concern for all of God's creatures, human and otherwise.

Thus says the Lord . . . you shall nurse and be carried on her arm, and dandled on her knees. As a mother comforts her child, so I will comfort you. (Isaiah 66:12–13)

Mother us, Beloved.

Courage of a Lifetime

An inquiring photographer once asked people, "What took the most courage for you?" Some of the replies were extraordinary.

One young man spoke of the courage it took to leave his homeland because of repression.

Another told of the courage needed to take up street preaching.

Still another cited the courage needed to take a complaint about an unjust dismissal to his union. It took courage, he said, because nobody encouraged him. He was alone.

That's generally the case when courage is needed.

Be a source of strength for others who need courage to do what is right. Pray for them and yourself and never stop relying on God's strength.

Cast your burden on the Lord, and He will sustain you. (Psalm 55:22)

Be my strength and courage, God.

Powerful Pollutants

How many pollutants are in your house? Perhaps more than you think.

- Paint, disposed of as a liquid, pollutes groundwater sources through seepage.
- Aerosol gases add to the ozone destroying gases in the atmosphere.
- Oil improperly disposed of also pollutes the groundwater.
- Pesticides retain their potency for many years.

What should you do if you have to dispose of something toxic? Contact your local health department. If there is no disposal program available to you, maybe it's time for you to get involved in protecting your world.

It's your environment — and your children's and, hopefully, their children's. Take responsibility. Take action.

The earth is the Lord's and all that is in it. (Psalm 24:1)

Remind us, Creator, that we are stewards of what You have made.

Careful with Praise

We know that praise from adults can help children, but psychologists tell us inappropriate praise can also hurt them.

Suppose a Little League baseball player who usually swings and misses hits a foul ball. "Good try" is sincere and appropriate praise. But a comment like "that's terrific!" sends the message that you don't think the child is capable of playing well.

Too much praise for good grades can make grades seem more important than what is learned.

And remember that praise for specific tasks, such as "You did a good job of putting together that puzzle," will mean more than a comment like "You're a smart girl."

Encourage children by praising their efforts, but be sure your praise is sincere and constructive. And don't forget that adults can use a kind word as well.

Let another praise you. (Proverbs 27:2)

I like others to praise me, Lord. Help me praise them, too, for we all need affirmation.

Planning Meetings that Work

It won't surprise anyone who has attended many meetings that they have been described as a place where people get together to talk about what they should already be doing.

Useful meetings require planning. That goes for community, social and church groups as well as for business.

If it's your responsibility, ask yourself what the problem is and who can offer information. There's no reason to invite more people than can contribute. An agenda can be valuable as a guideline.

Keep participants focused on the issues, keep things moving and keep things brief. Success in any activity calls for thinking and planning – from start to finish.

The will of the Lord shall prosper.
(Isaiah 53:10)

That Your will, my God, may be effective in my life.

The Quality of Mercy

The works of William Shakespeare are quoted on an amazing variety of subjects because of their wisdom and beauty. These are his most famous words on mercy. Read them, say them as though it were the first time:

> The quality of mercy is not strained.
> It droppeth as the gentle rain from heaven upon the place beneath.
> It is twice blest: It blesseth him that gives and him that takes.
> 'Tis mightiest in the mightiest. Mercy is an attribute of God Himself . . .
> Earthly power does show like God's when mercy seasons justice.

That's from Portia's speech in *The Merchant of Venice.* You may benefit from contemplating those words. You know Jesus said, "Blessed are the merciful for they shall receive mercy." Is there anyone who needs your mercy today?

The Lord is merciful . . . abounding in steadfast love. (Psalm 103:8)

May I be merciful as You are, Lover of Souls.

Career Considerations

If you have young people in your life who are trying to make career decisions, you might want to share these suggestions with them.

- Think about what matters to your head and your heart.
- Talk about careers with your parents.
- Volunteer or do internships in different careers as a way of gaining knowledge.
- Discuss possible careers with your guidance counselor.
- Ask school officials to bring in speakers from different careers.
- Use the local library for research in fields that interest you.
- Ask teachers, counselors and friends to help you evaluate your interests and abilities.
- Pray for the grace to know what you are meant to do in this life.

Then make a decision. But know that your career decision might change with time. Prepare for your career, but stay flexible. And give it your all.

Give [me] . . . understanding . . . that I may discern between good and evil. (I Kings 3:9)

Holy Spirit, enlighten me.

Enduring Criticism

Criticism. It's a word with a lot of negative connotations. Listening to criticism and putting it into perspective is hard for most of us.

Here's a quote that just might help you: "I do the very best I can, I mean to keep going. If the end brings me out all right, then what is said against me won't matter. If I'm wrong, ten angels swearing I was right won't make a difference."

That piece of wisdom was framed on the office wall of British statesman Winston Churchill. The words were said by President Abraham Lincoln.

Somehow it seems fitting that a leader who guided his bitterly divided country through the turmoil of a civil war could inspire another leader through the bleak days of a world war.

Follow their example. Do your best. That's all anyone can ask of you. Even yourself.

If the humble person slips, they even criticize him; he talks sense, but is not given a hearing. (Sirach 13:22)

When subject to criticism, Lord, remind me of Lincoln's example of courage under criticism.

Alone with God

"Language has created the word loneliness to express the pain of being alone, and the word solitude to express the glory of being alone." This comment by theologian Paul Tillich points out how much our feelings color our experience.

To be lonely is to feel isolated — cut off from others and locked into ourselves. It is to feel loss and sadness and self-pity.

But to experience solitude is to be alone with something, such as a book or music — or with God, in meditation or prayer. It is to feel peace and well-being.

To turn loneliness into solitude, we need to concentrate on something outside ourselves. That's why prayer can free us from isolation. It connects us with the beautiful and the universal, with God.

O my God, I cry by day, but You do not answer; and by night, but find no rest. Yet You are enthroned on the praises of Israel. In You our ancestors . . . trusted, and You delivered them. (Psalm 22:2–4)

When the "lonelies" come, God my companion, console me.

The "Easy Drift"

Margaret Payne, an ordained Lutheran pastor, confesses that all her life "pondering" has been one of her favorite activities.

Elementary and high school teachers said she was day-dreaming. A college instructor called her lazy and inattentive.

But Pastor Payne has discovered that she was "warming up for . . . mystical journeying that leads a human spirit to ledges of insight and occasionally to mountaintops of revelation."

This "easy drift of the spirit," opens minds and hearts to God by allowing Him "options to join us here or there" and guide us in His Will.

Pondering enables us to discover God's will by musing on "the normal happenings of normal days" until they begin to speak of God's will.

It helps us discover how to give ourselves to God in humility, prayer, listening, and yet more pondering over a lifetime.

Pondering – it's the active cultivation of an intimate relationship with God.

Mary treasured all these words and pondered them in her heart. (Luke 2:19)

Jesus, help us to value and practice being, listening, pondering, and caring.

Why Pray?

In the fourth century Gregory of Nyssa said that prayer enables us to forget injuries, overcome envy, defeat injustice, and atone for sin. It also refreshes and comforts us and gives us delight and solace. Finally, according to Gregory, "prayer is intimacy with God and contemplation of the invisible."

In the intervening centuries you can find many other, often eloquently phrased, reasons for prayer.

In the twentieth century, writer Madeleine L'Engle said that "in prayer the stilled voice learns to hold its peace, to listen with the heart to silence that is joy, is adoration." She goes on to say that the "time of contemplation . . . breaks time, breaks words, breaks me," while leaving her "in silence . . . healed and mended."

Challenge yourself to uncover your reasons to pray. And to abide in prayer.

"Lord, teach us to pray, as John taught his disciples." (Luke 11:1)

May I abide with You as You abide with me, Lord Christ.

How to Cheer Your Spouse

Here are some suggestions for pleasing your spouse — and yourself.

- Create your own special holiday, maybe the anniversary of your first date.
- Become your spouse's cheerleader when he/she has had a horrible day.
- Tell your spouse, "I love you," and really mean it.
- Sit on the same side of a restaurant booth.
- Share an intimate conversation away from family chaos.
- Do something your spouse thinks you've forgotten.
- Drop everything and do something for the one you love — *now!*

Whatever you do, do something special for your spouse and you'll be doing something special for your marriage and your mutual happiness.

I am my beloved's and my beloved is mine.
(Song of Solomon 6:3)

Loving Lord, You have given spouses to each other as best of friends, loving companions on life's journey. Help them to cherish and nourish that friendship.

Finding the Right Course

A moth normally uses the light of either the sun or the moon to guide itself as it flies. It keeps to a straight course by following a path such that the rays of the sun or moon always strike its eye at the same angle.

But sometimes a moth makes the mistake of trying to use a light such as a candle to guide it. Then keeping the light at an eighty-degree angle leads it not on a straight path but in a spiral. This takes it right into the flame.

You're also on the wrong course when you seek to find your way through drugs. Instead of leading to happiness, addiction ends in destruction. But there are steps you can take to get off that fatal path.

It is never too late to change direction.

Stand firm, therefore, and do not submit again to a yoke of slavery. (Galatians 5:1)

Give me, Jesus, the courage never to compromise Your gift of freedom.

An Optimist's Eye-View

Robert Louis Stevenson was the popular and prolific author of such enduring classics as *Treasure Island, Dr Jekyll and Mr. Hyde* and *A Child's Garden of Verses.*

The Scottish writer was also an optimist. He had had tuberculosis for years before dying while only in his forties. But Stevenson worked at keeping a positive attitude. Once, after a severe coughing spell, his wife commented, "I expect you still believe it's a wonderful day." His response, "I do. I will never permit a row of medicine bottles to block my horizon."

It's so easy to let something block your horizon. To let pain, fear, hatred, illness or even another person come between you and a spirit of hope-filled faith that allows an optimistic outlook.

Don't let anyone or anything control your attitude. Do all you can to maintain your physical, emotional and spiritual health and optimism. And, trust in God.

In trust shall be your strength. (Isaiah 30:15)

Jesus, help me to care for myself even as I trust in You.

Unplug the Bad News

Did you know that the more you watch or listen to the news on radio and television, the more pessimistic you become? News junkies have an exaggerated fear of the dangers around them.

Psychologist Jennifer James offers a strategy for keeping things in perspective. "To reduce stress, simply turn off your TV and radio, and go easy on the news magazines . . . You don't have to tune out forever, just take a rest," she suggests. "Anxiety, even if it is manufactured anxiety, can make us very cranky."

Now, no one is suggesting that you shouldn't stay well-informed. Ignorance is definitely not bliss. But it's easy to overdo anything, to put too much emphasis on something – even something that's basically good.

The world can be a tough place. But God made it our mission to make it better. And that should be good news.

The heavens are the Lord's heavens, but the earth He has given to human beings. (Psalm 115:16)

Creator, show us how to be good stewards of the Earth, Your gift to us.

Giving Youngsters Tools for Success

Walter J. Turnbull founded The Boys Choir of Harlem mainly to help youngsters build self-esteem and confidence. Today it's an internationally famous Choir, but its purpose remains unchanged.

Choir members, who range in age from ten to eighteen, must practice at least two hours a day. Turnbull emphasizes the importance of setting a goal and sticking to it. He points out that the self-discipline the youngsters learn "is transferable to everything else they do."

"We're much more than a choir," he says. "We're dedicated to helping children be successful. Music has the power to build their self-esteem."

Teaching young people to respect themselves is indeed essential to their success in life. Don't let a day go by without building up the confidence of a youngster or an adult who really needs it.

My child, honor yourself with humility, and give yourself the esteem you deserve. Who will acquit those who condemn themselves? And who will honor those who dishonor themselves? (Sirach 10:28–29)

Master, remind youth workers and teachers to respect each child in their charge.

A First Lady's Lessons on Life

Eleanor Roosevelt was a prolific writer and much-traveled speaker as well as the wife and later widow of America's thirty-second president, Franklin D. Roosevelt.

She once said that she had "never given very deep thought to a philosophy of life, though I have a few ideas that I think are useful to me."

Mrs. Roosevelt continued, "One is that you do whatever comes your way to do as well as you can, and another is that you think as little as possible about yourself and as much as possible about other people and about things that are interesting.

"The third is that you get more joy out of giving joy to others and should put a good deal of thought into the happiness that you are able to give."

Mrs. Roosevelt was right. The best gift you can give yourself may well be thinking of others, doing for others. It just might be the start of a better life.

The Lord is compassionate and merciful. (James 5:11)

Remind me, Savior, to make love of God and neighbor the basis of all my deeds.

Unforgettable Feasts

Holidays and other special occasions are often celebrated with elaborate feasts. Here are two that made the Guinness Book of Records.

The world's largest dish is served at Bedouin wedding feasts. To prepare it, cooked eggs are stuffed into fish; the fish are stuffed into cooked chickens; the chickens stuffed into a roasted sheep; and the sheep stuffed into a roasted camel!

The most lavish banquet on record was held in Iran in 1971. The menu included such items as quails' eggs stuffed with caviar, and roast peacock stuffed with foie gras. One of the wines served was Chateau Lafite-Rothschild 1945, at $160 a bottle.

Celebrations don't have to include such elaborate feasts. Actually, celebrations need not include any elaborate feast. The one ingredient is a joyful heart.

The people rejoiced greatly and celebrated.
(I Maccabees 7:48)

Whatever the occasions, Lord , help us rejoice and celebrate with a joy-filled heart.

Grass Roots Campaign for Safety

Nadine Milford went into shock when her daughter Melanie and three little grandchildren were killed by a drunk driver. In her pain, she asked God what to do.

The bereaved woman decided to fight for stricter laws and penalties for driving while intoxicated. And she didn't let the fact that she had no advocacy experience stop her. With friends and supporters she traveled sixty miles a day to lobby state legislators. They won.

New Mexico's attorney general said that "the accident galvanized public opinion in a way that we had never seen before . . . Nadine organized a grass roots campaign that made a real impact."

Nadine Milford admits that she often wanted to go home and just "pull the sheets over my head." But above anything else, she wanted the deaths of her daughter and grandchildren to have meaning. With her help, they do.

How do you give your life meaning?

Is it lawful to do good or to do harm . . . to save life or to kill? (Mark 3:4)

Wisdom of the Father, inspire our efforts to protect the precious life You have given us.

Ignorance Leads to Violence

In the early nineteenth century, a Massachusetts man named Joseph Palmer was snubbed by his neighbors. Tradespeople refused to serve him. Townspeople threw stones at him. Palmer was once ambushed by four men who attempted to forcibly shave him. When he fought them off, he was arrested on a charge of "unprovoked assault" and jailed for a year.

The cause of all this hatred? Palmer wore a beard before beards had become fashionable in the United States.

It's hard to believe this could happen. Or is it? Think about the suspicions and animosities between people today because of differences in race, religion, customs, even dress and personal grooming.

There is nothing wrong with recognizing our differences. There is a great deal wrong with making them more important than what we human beings have in common as God's children – our common humanity and our equality before our Maker.

Hatred stirs up strife. (Proverbs 10:12)

You delight in diversity, Creator. Help us, too, to delight in what we don't have in common and in what we do.

"This Grace of Love"

Cardinal John Henry Newman wrote, "My God, the Paraclete, if I differ at all from the world, it is because You have chosen me . . . and have lit up the love of God in my heart. If I differ from Your saints, it is because I do not ask earnestly enough for Your grace, and for enough of it, and because I do not diligently improve what You have given me. Increase in me this grace of love."

You know, we could each make the same observations. But as Cardinal Newman knew, there is a solution.

We can find the oil of grace for our lamps if, like Cardinal Newman, we pray and pray and pray ceaselessly and confidently – with gratitude for what we have, with a joyful anticipation of the time given to prayer.

Our good God always gives to those who ask.

Jesus told them a parable about their need to pray always and not to lose heart. (Luke 18:1)

Inspire me to pray ceaselessly and with confidence, Holy Spirit.

Today Is for Dreaming

Florence Clifton worked hard to get a college degree and she finally got it sixty-two years after she first started school.

Clifton attended the University of California at Los Angeles (UCLA) between 1927 and 1931. She quit school just four credits shy of graduation to help her parents during the Depression. She always intended to return to school, but soon found herself occupied with work, marriage, and raising a family.

Fortunately, when she did decide to finish her baccalaureate at age eighty-three, UCLA reviewed her records and awarded her a retroactive degree.

Clifton said, "When you get up in your eighties, you start looking back at what you've done and what you wish you'd done."

Those are wise words. You're never too old to fulfill a dream.

How attractive is wisdom in the aged, and understanding and counsel. (Sirach 25:5)

May we fulfill our dreams at every age, Source and Sustainer of Life.

Problem Behind the Anger

The things we seem to be angry about are not always the things really bothering us.

An eleven-year-old boy screamed at his mother that she ought to get a better job, that he was tired of being poor. Since they were not poor, his mother knew that was not the real problem.

Then she noticed the broken light on his bike, and that his bike helmet was too big and wouldn't stay on. For months the busy mother had delayed taking care of these things. A talk with her son confirmed that it *was* things like these that were making him feel deprived. She immediately took steps to remedy them.

For good relationships, it's important that we discover the reasons behind our own anger and other people's, too. It's also important to defuse anger for the health of body, mind and soul.

Be quick to listen, slow to speak, slow to anger. (James 1:19)

Enable me to discover and understand the reasons for my anger, Holy Spirit.

Strong Principles

Bayard Rustin was one of America's best known civil rights activists and a proponent of non-violence.

A Quaker himself, he once synopsized the principles that guided him:

- Nonviolent tactics.
- Constitutional means.
- Democratic procedures.
- Respect for the human person.
- Belief that all people are one.

These principles served Rustin well over the years.

They provide a difficult, but sure guide for anyone who would like to effect social change. Democracy works best when we work at it and encourage others to do the same.

A harvest of righteousness is sown in peace for those who make peace. (James 3:18)

Author of peace, sow peace in my heart, in my country.

Small Cuts, Large Hurts

Ever wonder why superficial paper cuts often hurt more than serious cuts? The reason, doctors tell us, is that sensory nerve endings are close to the skin and are especially numerous on the hands. One square inch of skin on the hand contains about seventy-two feet of nerve fiber. So paper cuts irritate sensitive nerve endings. As a result, we feel pain out of proportion to the injury.

Similarly, small cutting remarks from those close to us also cause a disproportionate amount of pain because we are unusually sensitive to people we love and respect. An example: Knowing that his wife enjoyed watching the birds that visited their yard, a man decided to build a bird feeder as a surprise gift for her. He spent his free time designing it to hang from a tree in the yard.

His wife saw the bird feeder and said without thinking, "It's too big. It'll spoil the look of that corner." The expression on her husband's face showed her the pain her remark had caused.

The love of our family and friends brings with it the obligation not to hurt them through thoughtlessness or impatience. They trust us to be kind.

Do not seek your own advantage, but that of the other. (I Corinthians 10:24)

God, help me to be thoughtful towards family, friends, everyone.

Stretch Your Way to Success

The late world-acclaimed actress Helen Hayes used to tell an intriguing tale about her early days in the theater. A producer told her she could be great — if only she were four inches taller.

"So," said Miss Hayes, "I was pulled and stretched until I felt I was in a medieval torture chamber. I gained nary an inch — but my posture became military. I became the tallest five-foot woman in the world."

Her new posture gave Helen Hayes a new attitude: "My refusal to be limited enabled me to play Mary of Scotland, one of the tallest queens in history."

It's a good story to remember when facing any limitation. Try to change, to stretch your limits. But if that isn't possible, consider stretching your own attitude.

It could be your key to your success.

Do not worry about your life . . . or about . . . what you will wear. Is not life more than food, and the body more than clothing? (Matthew 6:25)

Help me, Creator, to accept myself as I am.

Fathers: Today's the Day

Being a parent has always had its difficult choices. Today, some fathers are finding out that even deciding to do their best can come too late.

One father and business executive recalls that "ten years ago I told my wife and children to just wait until I get established, and then I could spend some time with them. Now that I want to get involved with them, I am finding they are more comfortable without me."

Rabbi Harold Kushner agrees. The well-known author says, "Some of the saddest people I know are men . . . who tell their teenage children, 'I've had my priorities wrong. . . . From now on, I'll be spending less time at work and more time with you,' only to be told, 'Gee, Dad, that's nice, but we have other plans.'"

Spend time with your children. Make the time to be a good father and a good husband. You will gain more than you can imagine.

The Lord honors a father above his children, and He confirms a mother's right over her children. (Sirach 3:2)

Inspire fathers to put their wives and children first, Father of all. And remind their families to show their appreciation.

Share Learning and Caring

The late David and Dovetta Wilson are examples of the good influence parents can have.

Mr. and Mrs. Wilson both grew up in poor families and never went past elementary school. But both of them worked to see to it that their own nine children were educated.

They also showed their children the importance of giving to others. The children remember that their mother always had a good hot meal for anybody – friend or stranger – who needed it.

And they remember that their father's last advice to them was to give something back to their community.

The children, now college graduates and professionals, established a scholarship fund to honor their parents. It has helped dozens of students go to college.

An appreciation for learning is one of the most valuable gifts parents can give their children. Add a spirit of compassion and young people will be on their way to a happy and fulfilling life.

An educated person knows many things, and one with much experience knows what he is talking about. (Sirach 34:9)

Help us to seek learning for ourselves and encourage it for others, Spirit of God.

Routine Breakers

In a rut? Consider these suggestions for breaking monotonous routines.

- Worship at a church or synagogue noted for its glorious music and liturgies.
- Write a letter to a far-away friend.
- Turn off the radio, TV and stereo. Enjoy the silence for a few days.
- Play tourist in the nearest big city — even if it's your own.
- Give a co-worker a sincere compliment.
- Be kind to a "difficult" person in your life.
- Laugh.
- Walk or jog on a new route.
- Visit a sick or aged neighbor at home, in the hospital or in a nursing home.

It's the little things, the simple, free or inexpensive things that add variety to life. Jot down a list of your own ideas. Then start to act on them.

Commit your way to the Lord; trust in Him, and He will act. (Psalm 37:5)

I do commit my way to You, Lord. Deliver me from monotonous routine.

Docking in a Desert

Back in 1868, a devastating earthquake triggered a fifty-foot ocean wave off the Peruvian coast. This massive wave swept over a ship anchored offshore. Instead of sinking, the ship rode the crest of the wave and was carried two miles inland.

Miraculously, no one on board was killed, but crew members were astonished to find that their ship was sitting in the middle of the Atacama desert!

While the ship was not damaged, it was hopelessly grounded.

Life is like that sometimes. We experience an upheaval in our lives, like losing a job, and feel hopelessly run aground, out of our element. It's easy to forget the main facts: we survive, we have family, friends, God. In time, there will be another job.

Meanwhile — always — keep your confidence in your God and yourself.

"Your Father in heaven [will] give good things to those who ask Him." (Matthew 7:11)

Father, strengthen my trust in Your loving care for me.

Guide to Contented Living

The famed German writer Goethe offered a list of nine requisites for contented living. They are as timely now as they were when he wrote them two hundred years ago.

"Health enough to make work a pleasure. Wealth enough to support your needs. Strength enough to battle with difficulties and overcome them.

"Grace enough to confess your sins and forsake them. Patience enough to toil until some good is accomplished. Charity enough to see some good in your neighbor.

"Love enough to move you to be useful to others. Faith enough to make real the things of God. Hope enough to remove all anxious fears concerning the future."

Goethe showed wisdom in these thoughts, perhaps especially in the use of the word "enough." Often we seek something more when contentment — and gratitude —can come from having enough.

There is great gain in godliness with contentment; for we brought nothing into the world, so that we can take nothing out of it (1 Timothy 6:6–7)

Grace me with contentment, Jesus, for in having You I do have everything — and more.

Sharing the Fruits of a Garden

Here's an idea for all you gardeners out there. Check with your church or synagogue to see if there's a small piece of ground that could be turned into a community vegetable garden.

That's what a group of older people in Auburn, Maine, did. Now they have a thriving enterprise.

In fact, so much is being grown that there's a table in the church with a sign on it saying "give and receive." Gardeners leave their surplus produce there. Those who take something leave baked goods and preserves in return.

Neighbors come a little closer to one another because of the sharing. People feel less needy when they can give in turn.

Sharing sets off chain reactions of lasting consequences. Begin with small things. Find ways to share. You'll be the richer for it because bonds of friendship will grow and friendship is the most precious gift.

God loves a cheerful giver. (2 Corinthians 9:7)

What neighbor or what organization needs my generosity, God?

True Generosity of Self

Birthdays, anniversaries, holidays, there are lots of occasions when we want to give presents. Make your gifts to friends and relatives something to improve their well being, advises columnist Jane Brody.

She suggests some gifts that promote health or make life easier. For instance, membership in a fitness center, or an exercise video.

To make cooking easier, you could give a small microwave oven or an electric can-opener.

If people have special needs, plan accordingly. For someone on a restricted diet, you might get an assortment of appropriate foods. For a person who lives alone, consider bringing in a meal once a week. Or extend an invitation to dinner once a month.

Gifts such as these show that you really care about the person. The value of any one of these gifts, as with all gifts, is measured in love.

Does not a word surpass a good gift? Both are to be found in a gracious person. (Sirach 18:17)

Make me sincere, Giver of every good gift.

Community = Hospitality

Would you like to improve the quality of life in your neighborhood? Be more hospitable and gracious.

- Invite someone who lives alone to your house for a holiday meal or take them with you on an outing.
- Welcome the newcomer on your block by providing refreshments on move-in day.
- Be aware of neighborhood events, such as a new baby or illness or death in a family. Make yourself available for errands, chores, or child-care.
- Welcome your children's friends, offering them snacks when they come to play or study or listen to music.

Hospitality is the art of being gracious. Like any art, graciousness can be learned. Learn it and you will find that you, too, will have a wonderful time.

Do not neglect to show hospitality . . . by doing that some have entertained angels without knowing it. (Hebrews 13:2)

May hospitality be the salt of my life, Gracious God.

Making a Day of Rest

Jesus said that the "Sabbath was made for humankind." Our challenge is to own our Sabbath.

Begin the evening before by greeting the sunset. On your Sabbath greet the dawn. Be alert to the expectancy of those holy hours of sunset and dawn. Marvel at Creation. Then notice the Sabbath's sunset.

Try to make your Sabbath a day at your disposal. Study the Scriptures. Attend religious services, if possible as a family. Include enjoyment of art – Dante called it "almost God's grandchild" – and music in your Sabbath leisure.

Savor good food and good company at relaxed meals. Be joyful. Play.

But mostly, r-e-l-a-x in that present moment which is the Sabbath, the Lord's day.

Remember the Sabbath day, and keep it holy. (Exodus 20:8)

Savior, help me keep Your day.

Keep Your Strengths — Strong

It's natural for people to emphasize their strong points. But, strengths taken to extremes can turn into problems.

Hollywood producer Dore Schary had this to say: "A person who calls himself frank and candid can very easily find himself becoming tactless and cruel. A person who prides himself on being tactful can find eventually that he has become evasive and deceitful.

"A person with firm convictions can become pigheaded. A person who is inclined to be temperate and judicious can sometimes turn into someone with weak convictions . . . Loyalty can lead to fanaticism. Caution can become timidity. Freedom can become license. Confidence can become arrogance. Humility can become servility.

"All these are ways in which strength can become weakness."

There's much truth here. Think about it. And be careful that your strengths don't become weaknesses.

"My grace is sufficient for you, for power is made perfect in weakness." (2 Corinthians 12:9)

May we, by relying on You, God, be strong.

Small Obligations

Just how important are little acts of generosity?

When you're simply thinking about a cheery greeting, a quick errand, a pat on the back for a job well done, they do indeed seem like small things.

But when you're the person receiving that attention they can mean everything. When someone goes out of the way to pay attention to us it makes us feel good about ourselves, about the person who cared and about the world in general. And being the giver can make us feel pretty good, too — both useful and appreciated.

Sir Humphry Davy was a scientist, a pioneer in electrochemistry. He also showed he knew a lot about people when he said: "Life is made up, not of great sacrifices and duties, but of little things in which smiles and kindnesses and small obligations are what win the heart and secure comfort."

Sacrifice and offering You do not desire; but You have given me an open ear. . . . I delight to do Your will, O my God. (Psalm 40:6, 8)

Give us a genuine delight in the many tiny daily sacrifices required for a whole-souled obedience to You, Jesus.

Ground Rules
for Marital Conflict

Conflict. No matter how hard couples try, eventually there are disputes in every marriage. They can be over anything from money to television to sex to jealousy. Most conflicts are minor, but it's how you solve them that may determine the quality of your marriage. One counselor made these suggestions:

Set the ground rules for open discussion together. Talk about how you would like to handle problems. Say what's on your mind. And be sure to listen carefully. Resolve problems day-to-day while they are fresh. How you handle small, everyday issues will influence how you handle the larger ones when they come.

Forgive. Everyone makes mistakes. The challenge is to forgive. Don't keep count. Make sure you choose the proper time and place for forgiveness: a walk before dinner, or a drive to a nearby park. Make it a firm promise to always forgive each other before going to sleep. Be willing to see where you are wrong. Be ready to be first to say, "I'm sorry."

Be gentle, be kind, be loving.

Be angry, but do not sin; do not let the sun go down on your anger. (Ephesians 4:26)

Jesus, teach me to be gentle, patient and kind. Give me the ability to respond tenderly to apologies.

"Know Yourself"

How well do you understand yourself?

Philosophers have long urged people to make an effort to consider and learn just what makes them tick. An inscription on the temple of Apollo at Delphi, Greece, reads, "Know thyself." Socrates said that "the unexamined life is not worth living." And Lao Tzu, the founder of Taoism, explained:

It is wisdom to know others;
It is enlightenment to know one's self.
The conqueror of men is powerful;
The master of himself is strong.
It is wealth to be content;
It is willful to force one's way on others.
Endurance is to keep ones place;
Long life is to die and not perish.

Self-knowledge shows us ourselves as we really are. It can teach us both humility and self-esteem. And it can bring us closer to the person God means us to be.

The truth will make you free. (John 8:32)

Come, Holy Spirit, come teach me to know myself and so to grow in humility and self-esteem.

Choosing What's Right and Difficult

Most of us like to see ourselves as people of integrity. But do you ever wonder how you would act if you were put to the test?

Reuben Gonzales more than made the grade. He was in the final match of a major racquetball tournament and looking for his first professional win.

At match point in the final game Gonzales made a super show for the victory. The referee and a linesman called it good. But the almost champion saw it differently. Declaring that his shot had hit the floor before it skipped into the wall, he shook his opponent's hand and walked off the court.

Asked why he did it, Reuben Gonzales simply said, "It was the only thing I could do to maintain my integrity."

Honor and honesty can command a high price. That's why they are worth so much.

Pursue peace with everyone, and the holiness without which no one will see the Lord. (Hebrews 12:14)

Thanks for the example of Your holy women and men of integrity and virtue, God.

Lonely Seeker of Comfort

A woman from Halifax, Nova Scotia, described her experience when she went to a local church for the first time. A widow, she moved to a smaller house in a new town where she found herself overwhelmed by loneliness.

She hadn't been to church since she was a little girl, but hoped she might find solace. There wasn't a crowd at the service and everyone seemed to know and talk to everyone else.

Because the newcomer didn't know the liturgy, she kept glancing at others to see if she was standing or kneeling at the right times. At the end, she walked slowly back down the aisle, hoping someone would say hello. They didn't. Even "the Vicar was shaking hands with people . . . but somehow I seemed to get missed."

Don't let someone "get missed."

Reach out. It can be as simple as a smile and a word of welcome. We need one another.

What does the Lord require of you but to do justice, and to love kindness. (Micah 6:8)

You've never ignored me, Lord. May I never ignore anyone.

The Truth about Equality

The American Declaration of Independence declares that "that all men are created equal." Yet discrimination was widespread and slavery was permitted by custom and law.

As late as 1820, the Maryland state constitution required office-holders to be professed Christians. Non-Christians could not hold office without denying their faith. But in the 1820s, the Maryland legislature began debating the merits and validity of this provision. In the forefront of the struggle to eliminate it was Thomas Kennedy. Kennedy told fellow legislators, "There are few Jews in the United States; in Maryland there are very few. But if there were only one – to that one we ought to do justice."

The struggle for equality is on-going. This is why minorities still need to press for their civil rights.

Examine your own attitudes and actions and change those which keep you from treating others as equal. You will advance the cause of freedom. Harry S. Truman said, "We believe that all . . . are created in the image of God."

You shall not wrong or oppress a resident alien. . . . You shall not abuse any widow or orphan. . . . If you do abuse them, when they cry out to me, I will surely hear their cry. (Exodus 22:21–23)

May our lives testify that everyone is created in Your image and likeness, Creator Lord.

Waspish, But Wonderful

Do wasps, those nasty, stinging, buzzing, seemingly always angry insects have any use — other than giving us itchy red welts or allergic reactions?

Gardeners and farmers know that the answer is a resounding "yes." Fruit-bearing fig trees as well as ornamental ones rely on specific species of wasp for pollination. No wasps, no sweet, juicy figs. No beautiful fig trees either.

Other wasps prey on worms which attack corn, cotton, soybeans, tomatoes and potatoes. Wheat, oats, barley and lima beans are protected by still other species of wasp.

Gypsy moths and some other insects that weaken or destroy trees are also attacked by certain types of wasps.

Wasps. Yes, they buzz and sting. But they also guard our food crops, protect and pollinate trees.

Nothing was created by God without a purpose.

"I know the plans I have for you, says the Lord, plans for your welfare and not for harm, to give you a future with hope." (Jeremiah 29:11)

Help us treasure everything You've created, Lord.

Putting Theory to Work

Rooted in a belief in God and a theory of natural law that can be traced back to Aristotle, the U. S. Declaration of Independence is more than a great historical document. Here is what Woodrow Wilson had to say about it: "The Declaration of Independence . . . is of no consequence . . . unless we can translate its general terms into . . . the present day. . . . It is an eminently practical document . . . not a theory of government, but a program of action."

The Declaration is unique in that it links equality and human rights. "All men are created equal." But more than that, "they are endowed by their Creator with certain unalienable rights, that among these are life, liberty and the pursuit of happiness." Do you claim these rights for yourself but deny them to others, or simply not care if others have those rights? We in America have done that often. Still, the test is not whether we as a nation are perfect, but whether we are progressing toward equal rights.

Progress requires "a program of action," not just by our national, state and local governments but by we the citizens.

Those who look into . . . the law of liberty, and persevere, being not hearers . . . but doers . . . will be blessed in their doing. (James 1:25)

May I reflect on the truths we as a nation hold "self evident" and put them into action, Author of our liberty.

If You Don't Know
Where You're Going . . .

Baseball great Yogi Berra once said, "You've got to be careful if you don't know where you're going, because you might not get there." On another occasion, he warned, "If you don't know where you're going, you'll wind up somewhere else."

The logic may appear muddled, but their truth is clear. Unless we have a positive, worthwhile goal, life can become a series of wrong turns and dead-ends.

The everyday goals we set for ourselves are just steps toward our main goal in life: to use our God-given talents to fulfill our unique mission and make the world a better place.

There are as many different paths to this goal as there are people. But as long as we know where we are going, we can choose a path leading in the right direction.

O that my ways may be steadfast in keeping Your statutes! (Psalm 119:5)

When it is difficult to use my God-given talents for good, God, encourage me.

Age-Old Secret

A California botanist tried sprouting four of seven live lotus seeds found in an ancient lake bed in China. Then she used the radiocarbon method to age-date them. Unfortunately, it killed them. The oldest seed was about 1,200 years old.

A dozen years later, she age-dated the remaining three seeds with a new method that left them intact. She planted one of these seeds — a youngster only 332 years old — and it flourished, growing and putting out lots of leaves.

The secret of a lotus seed's vitality is thought to be an enzyme that keeps it from deteriorating with age as most seeds do.

For people, the secret of continued vitality in old age is less tangible. But staying interested and involved in the world around you may make all the difference in keeping your spirit flourishing a long, long time.

Old age is not honored for length of time, or measured by number of years; but understanding is gray hair for anyone, and a blameless life is ripe old age. (Wisdom of Solomon 4:8–9)

Bless men and women with the wisdom of many years, Holy Spirit.

The Power of Persistence

Just having the opportunity to show your talents can be a struggle. If you have had this problem, it may help to know you're in good company.

Johann Sebastian Bach, the great organist and composer, applied for the position of music director at St. Thomas Church, Leipzig, Germany. He was passed over. Only after two other applicants decided not to take it and the city had been without a music director for six months was Bach offered the position.

The problem: in spite of Bach's genius, he lacked the education, the college degree that was demanded. The Leipzig council finally hired him because he agreed to take on the extra tasks of teaching Latin and catechism.

When an opportunity is delayed, don't give up. Perseverance and patience are often rewarded, if only we don't give up.

The seed is the word of God . . . the good soil . . . ones who, when they hear the word, hold it fast in an honest and good heart, and bear fruit with patient endurance. (Luke 8:11, 15)

Jesus, prepare my heart to receive Your Word. Teach me Your patience.

Remembering a Hero

The students of Virgil Grissom Junior High School in South Ozone Park, New York, refused to let a nineteenth century black hero be forgotten.

The students conducted a letter-writing campaign to the Coast Guard, politicians and the media to honor Captain Mike Healy, a skipper who sailed along the Alaskan coast from 1886 to 1895. Born to a slave mother, Healy helped sailors who were trapped in the icy waters and transported reindeer from Siberia to Alaska, where they were used for food and clothing by sick and starving Eskimos.

Inspired by his story, 130 students wrote nearly eight hundred letters. The Coast Guard named a polar-class ice-breaker – the largest ship in the Coast Guard fleet – after Captain Healy.

These young people used a simple yet effective tool to ensure that a special man was remembered.

Perhaps, there's a letter you have been meaning to write. Make time to write it today. It might do more good than you can imagine.

His fame spread far. (2 Chronicles 26:15)

Remind me, Jesus, that I will be remembered for the good I do, the love I give.

Part of the Whole

Amish people maintain a simple way of life. They believe that being "plain folk" is best and use modern technology only when absolutely necessary.

Because of this attitude, the Amish have great respect for one another. Every member of their community, from the youngest child to the most experienced elder, is necessary. They depend upon each person to do some particular job in order for the entire group to survive.

In many ways, the same is true for us if we only stop to think about it. Whether we live in a small community or a major city, each man, woman and young person has a part to play in helping the whole community to function at its best.

Don't be tempted to say, "What difference can I possibly make?" No one else has your special talents, outlook, opportunities. You are irreplaceable to God's plan.

**The unfolding of Your words gives light.
(Psalm 119:130)**

Holy Spirit, teach me to make a difference by the way I live my life.

Deceptions, Harmless and Otherwise

Menthol is cooling, right? Wrong!

The temperature of menthol shaving cream is no lower than the temperature of any other shaving cream. And menthol cough drops don't make your mouth any cooler. Menthol tricks the receptors in the skin or mouth that tell the brain they're feeling something cool.

But at least this deception is harmless. The same cannot be said for the effects of addictive drugs. These drugs also fool the brain. They give a false sense of euphoria and well-being. Problems seem unimportant or non-existent. But using drugs not only fails to remedy problems, it creates new ones.

Don't let yourself or a loved one be seduced by drugs. If you need help, ask for it. If you know someone with a problem, encourage him or her to find help.

Don't pretend everything is all right if it isn't. You are only deceiving yourself.

No one ever hates his own body, but he nourishes and tenderly cares for it. (Ephesians 5:29)

How can I better care for myself today so as to give You praise, Holy God?

Keep Your Faith and Goals Fixed

Florence Chadwick earned her place in the record books by being the first woman to swim the English Channel in both directions.

Yet in her next quest she nearly defeated herself. In 1952, she set out from Catalina Island, intent on reaching the fog shrouded California coast, twenty-one miles away. Numbed by cold and fatigue and unable to see the foggy shore, she gave up fifteen hours later. She didn't realize she was within a half-mile of her goal.

Florence Chadwick later admitted that it was her inability to keep sight of her goal that made her quit. Two months later, she tried again. The cold, the fatigue and the fog still plagued her. But this time she kept faith with herself. The first woman to accomplish this feat, Florence Chadwick also bested the men's record by two hours.

Set your own goal. And never give up. You may be closer than you think.

Do not, therefore, abandon that confidence of yours; it brings a great reward. For you need endurance, so that when you have done the will of God, you may receive what was promised. (Hebrews 10:35–36)

Shore-up our confident endurance in times of trial, Redeemer.

Creating an Atmosphere

Our attitudes and outlook affect the atmosphere around us the way the way earth's atmosphere affects the sunlight. Sunlight is made up of all colors. But the atmosphere scatters the blue light waves (which are short) more than the red ones and others (which are longer). And since it is mostly blue light waves that bounce off the atmosphere and reach our eyes, the sky looks blue.

In the same way, we color other people's view of life. People who are enthusiastic have an encouraging effect on those around them; those who are pessimistic tend to dishearten others.

Kind, loving parents produce an atmosphere of trust, affection, and self-confidence; those who are harsh or uncaring, an atmosphere that stunts the emotional growth of their children.

Try to reflect positive attitudes that help others see life's blue skies.

**I have continued My faithfulness to you.
(Jeremiah 31:3)**

May we, in memory of Your love and faithfulness, Lord, be loving and faithful in all things.

Fast Learners Take Off

A family of birds called mound builders are found in Australia and on certain South Sea islands. They build their nests on high mounds of soil and leaves. And unlike other birds, they hatch fully feathered and able to fly.

Mound builders are an exception to the rule. Most young birds grow feathers as they mature. They learn to use their wings only gradually – with lots of flapping and faltering starts, and crash landings.

New skills that we develop and ventures we undertake are rather like learning to fly. They take time and practice. We can't expect to get it right the first time.

Failures are part of learning.

Be patient, therefore, beloved, until the coming of the Lord. The farmer waits for the precious crop, being patient with it until it receives the early and the late rain. You also must be patient. (James 5:7)

Enable me to bear my failures with patience, Lord of the Harvest.

The Earliest Age

Cato the Elder, an accomplished orator and writer, was also a Roman statesman.

When he was over eighty years old, he started to study Greek. Someone asked him why he began such a hard undertaking at his age.

Cato answered, "It's the earliest age I have left."

Too many of us spend time thinking it's too late: too late to learn, too late to play, too late to change. Strangely enough, it is apparently never too late or too early to make excuses for ourselves.

Each day of your life brought you to where you are and who you are today. Take advantage of your past and learn from it. Then consider how you can best use today – and tomorrow.

The earliest age you have left is *now*.

Like a drop of water from the sea and a grain of sand, so are a few years among the days of eternity. (Sirach 18:10)

Holy Wisdom, may I live today as if it were my first and my last day.

Away for the Weekend

Getting away for the weekend might be the best thing for a friendship. In the course of everyday obligations, the true intimacy of friendship can be lost.

A friend can be taken for granted. Familiarity can breed contempt. Obligations can take precedence, and a friendship can get "second best." We can forget the reasons we first became friends; the significance of the relationship.

A weekend at a lake, a forest, or a mountainside retreat can be just the change needed for refreshment, privacy and talk. Moments in front of a crackling fire or making a meal together can also relieve everyday stresses enough for you to recall your friend's uniqueness and see again in your friend and in nature the face of God.

Letting go, getting away, a change of pace are all simple ways to recharge a friendship. And while you are thinking about friendship, make the time to renew your friendship with God.

Just as water reflects the face, so one human heart reflects another. (Proverbs 27:19)

May I share Your love in my friendships, Jesus.

An Anonymous Opinion

There's no doubt that "Anonymous" can be very wise. Here are some Anonymous thoughts on people perhaps best known as "them" and "us."

When other people act badly, they're ugly. When you do it, it's nerves.

When they're set in their ways, they're obstinate. When you are, it's firmness.

When they don't like your friends, they're prejudiced. When you don't like theirs, you're simply showing good judgment.

When they try to be accommodating, they're apple-polishing. When you do it, you're using tact.

When they take time to do things, they're just slow. When you take ages, you're being deliberate.

When they find fault, they're cranky. When you do it you're extremely discerning.

Recognize those other people? How about yourself? Next time you talk about other people stop to think: would you say the same things about yourself?

Why do you see the speck that is in your neighbor's eye, but do not notice the log in your own eye? (Matthew 7:3)

Jesus, help me to be ever alert to the danger of judging others. Let me see and work on my own flaws first.

A Person, Not a Handicap

A dentist was upset when he first learned that his newborn son had Down's syndrome. But he quickly came to love his son as an individual, just as he did his other children.

He said, "I realized that we all have problems and handicaps of one kind or another." No longer feeling hopeless, he began thinking about how modern medicine and education could help his son.

"It won't be easy," he said, "but God gave us our son and will give us the strength and understanding to help him lead a happy life."

This baby boy will have one great advantage that some babies and children do not have, an abundance of love, encouragement and acceptance. If you are a parent, extend these to your children. If you are not, pray that parents will love, encourage and accept all their children. And try to lend practical support, too.

I took them up in my arms . . . I led them with cords of human kindness, with bands of love . . . I bent down to them and fed them. (Hosea 11:3–4)

Father, help parents love, encourage and accept all of their children.

A Guide to TV for Parents

Adults sometimes forget that youngsters don't see things in the same way that they do.

Fred Rogers has reason to remember. The host of the popular children's series *Mister Rogers' Neighborhood* says, "A young child came up to me one day and asked, 'How did you get out of the TV?' Ever since then I've been concerned with how to help children understand that television pictures are only pictures."

Pre-schoolers frequently blur fantasy and reality. So it's important for parents to set guidelines.

Watch along with children when you can. Discuss programs. Encourage youngsters to express opinions and develop their critical thinking.

Remember, too, the power of good example when it comes to watching, changing the channel, or turning off the set.

Jesus . . . said . . . "Let the little children come to Me; do not stop them for it is to such as these that the kingdom of God belongs." . . . And He took them up in His arms, laid His hands on them, and blessed them. (Mark 10:14, 16)

May we be good examples for our children, God.

A Shield Against Stress

Anybody who has ever had a painful sunburn knows how important it is to use sunscreen. Animals living in the Tropics also need some form of built-in sunscreen such as that provided by fur or feathers.

But how does the hippopotamus, with its bare pale skin, survive under the blazing African sun? For one thing, it feeds at night. During the day it spends most of its time up to its neck in water or mud. But since it has to keep its head above the water or mud, nature has provided a sunscreen for it. The glands of its skin secrete a reddish fluid that screens out ultraviolet rays.

Just as it's essential to protect our bodies from sunburns, it's also important to prevent ourselves from being burned emotionally by stress. The pressures, the conflicting needs, the problems that produce stress are part of life.

We need to recall that we are not alone, that God has a purpose for us and helps us toward that end. Knowing that God is with us in all circumstances, that God loves us, can give us emotional protection even in the most trying times.

Are not five sparrows sold for two pennies? Yet not one of them is forgotten in God's sight. . . . You are of more value than many sparrows. (Luke 12:6–7)

God, remind me that You are always with me.

The Meaning of Words

Cinderella's slippers may have been changed to glass by the sound of a single word.

Scholars point out that only in versions of the story derived from the French does Cinderella wear glass slippers. In other versions of the story around the world, her slippers were made of a more comfortable material: fur.

The story was told orally long before it was written. When Charles Perrault wrote down the story in the late seventeenth century, he probably mistook the old French word *vair,* meaning *ermine* for the word *verre,* meaning *glass.* The pronunciation is the same, though the meaning is different.

A word or two can often make a great difference. Words like "Thank you" and "I'm sorry" can change our relationship with others.

A soft answer turns away wrath, but a harsh word stirs up anger. (Proverbs 15:1)

Make my words gracious, Word of the Father.

A Distant Goal Achieved

One of the biggest sports upsets of the century was achieved by Billy Mills. Mills won the 10,000 meter race in the 1964 Summer Olympics.

Before he won the gold medal, he had run five 10,000 meter races at his Marine camp but had not won. Few in the sports world had heard of him and no one even expected him to finish among the top runners.

Mills was shoved off the track in the last lap by another runner. But he made an amazing sprint and flew past the two favored runners. Mills says now that he knew he could win the race, even though others were skeptical.

He speaks to youth groups about confidence and goalsetting. Where he grew up, he says, "No one I knew had goals, or a reason to live. Life was day to day. Kids in an environment like that, they don't know an opportunity when they see one."

Encourage yourself and those around you to recognize opportunities to do something worthwhile and to seize them.

Strive for the greater gifts. (I Corinthians 12:31)

Jesus, help me set and attain rewarding goals.

Life Saver at Sea

A life-or-death drama played out at sea during a whale-watching expedition. After the ship cleared the harbor, a tourist noticed a woman tinkering with the lock on a gate by the rail. Why would she want to open the gate? He watched for a few minutes and then spoke to the first mate. They both suspected that the woman was suicidal.

The tourist went over to her for what seemed like a casual chat and stayed with her for three and a half hours. The conversation confirmed what he had suspected: the woman was desperate and was actually planning to jump overboard.

A life was saved because someone had noticed and someone had listened. Don't be afraid to follow your intuition. If something feels wrong, it probably is.

Help the weak. (1 Thessalonians 5:14)

Give me the courage to follow my intuitions when helping others, Jesus.

Reflections on Thinking

The next time you have a problem to solve that does not yield to straightforward thinking, try lateral thinking instead.

Edward deBono of Oxford University advocates the use of "detours and reversals" to change perspective.

Here is an example: employees at a new skyscraper were upset because of long waits for elevators. They could have staggered work hours or scheduled the elevators to handle only certain floors during peak times. Instead, they installed mirrors around the elevators' entrances. That way people could look at themselves and one another. Since they were not bored, they didn't mind the wait.

That's problem-solving by lateral thinking.

Whatever is on your mind, do not be afraid to try new approaches to your decision-making. It helps to think both clearly and creatively.

I will decide what to do. (Exodus 33:5)

Inspire my decision-making, Holy Spirit.

Unclear Ads

Have you ever been puzzled by a TV commercial that didn't seem to have a point – that was just a lot of images flashed on the screen, accompanied by pounding music? If so, you have lots of company.

A recent survey showed that these quick cuts, as they are called, do not work well. Viewers find it hard to absorb so many images and sounds in a short time.

The advertiser's message just doesn't come across as well as it does in commercials that have an obvious message, with fewer pictures and less obtrusive music.

Our lives, too, can become so fast-paced and filled with activity that they do not seem to have a clear focus. We may need to take stock and eliminate some of the unimportant activities that clutter our time and sap our energy so that we can concentrate on what we really want to accomplish.

[Jesus said,] "Come away to a deserted place all by yourselves and rest a while." (Mark 6:31)

Some parts of my life are far more important than others. Holy Spirit, when I get confused, please help me sort out one from the other.

Wrong Way — or Right?

"Wrong Way" Corrigan got his nickname back in 1938 when he left New York in his plane, heading for California, and ended up in Ireland.

Actually, it was no mistake. Charles Lindbergh was Douglas Corrigan's hero. Corrigan learned to fly and bought a little plane. He hoped to cross the Atlantic solo, as only Lindbergh and a few others had done at that time. But the Department of Commerce refused him permission for the flight. So he announced his plan to fly to California — and took off across the Atlantic instead.

The nickname "Wrong Way Corrigan" did not bother him. He knew the truth — and the value of a little publicity.

Belittling nicknames, on the other hand, can be devastating. Avoid nicknames or labels that hurt others. We are all entitled to our own good name.

Who, then, are you to judge your neighbor?
(James 4:12)

Enable me to accept myself, and those around me, "as is," God.

Advice for Parents and Other Adults

If you have teenagers in your life, you know both the problems and necessity of good communications. Here are a few suggestions from the young people of James Madison Memorial High School, Madison, Wisconsin:

- Praise us when we do well; and tell us you love us — even if we act as though we do not want to hear it.
- Let us form our own opinions, even if it means disagreeing with you.
- Be honest with us.
- Help us solve our problems, but don't solve them for us or we'll never grow up.
- Never stop talking to us.

That last point is essential for parents and all adults who really want to help teens grow. Do not give up on today's young people. Stay approachable, keep talking, keep listening.

A word is better than a gift. (Sirach 18:16)

Open parents' ears to their children's voices spoken and unspoken, Holy Spirit.

When Is a Fruit a Vegetable?

The causes of disagreements among people seem endless. The U.S. Supreme Court once adjudicated a dispute over whether the tomato is a fruit or a vegetable.

In the late nineteenth century, duty was charged on imported vegetables, but not on imported fruits. An importer brought tomatoes from the West Indies and had to pay duty. He protested that tomatoes were a fruit and took the case to the Supreme Court. The court ruled that since tomatoes were served at dinner, like vegetables, not at dessert, like fruits, they were legally vegetables.

Whatever the cause, there are peaceful ways of resolving conflicts. Not just legal disputes, but the inevitable small disagreements of everyday life:

- A husband wants to go to a baseball game, his wife wants to see a play.
- Two friends want to have dinner, one loves Italian food, the other Chinese.
- One person is uncomfortable in a cool office, an associate when it's warm.

Small differences can lead to strained relationships if those involved lose their tempers or *don't* try to understand each other with courtesy and respect.

The mind of the wise makes their speech judicious, and adds persuasiveness to their lips. Pleasant words are like a honeycomb, sweetness to the soul and health to the body. (Proverbs 16:23–24)

Jesus, be my model of courteous conflict resolution.

Sounds of Beauty

On a desolate island off the west coast of Scotland, the sand "sings" when it's touched. Walking across the beach produces a wide range of musical tones, like playing a musical instrument.

Scientists think the structure of the sand creates the sounds. The grains of sand are tiny pieces of quartz, rounded by the sea. Each grain is surrounded by a pocket of air. When the sand is touched, friction between the air and the grains produces musical tones.

We may not have a chance to hear the strange music of singing sand, but we all have a chance to hear the music of rustling leaves. Happiness need not be pursued in exotic places. The joyful music of God's Creation surrounds us.

All we need to do is listen.

The heavens are telling the glory of God; and the firmament proclaims His handiwork. (Psalm 19:1)

Open our ears, Creator, to hear the symphony of Your Creation.

Leading the Simple Life

"Our life is frittered away by detail," said nineteenth-century writer Henry David Thoreau. "Simplify, simplify. Instead of three meals a day, if it be necessary eat but one; instead of a hundred dishes, five; and reduce other things in proportion."

Thoreau simplified his own life by building a cabin in the woods near Walden Pond, in Concord, Massachusetts. He lived alone there for two years observing, studying, thinking and writing.

In his account of life at Walden, he tells us that he had three pieces of limestone on his desk, but when he realized that they had to be dusted every day, he threw them out the window in disgust. He refused the gift of a mat because he didn't want to waste time shaking it out. "I declined it, preferring to wipe my feet on the sod before my door," said Thoreau.

Not many of us would try to simplify our lives to that extent. But most of us could get rid of excess baggage: unnecessary chores, like the upkeep of something we never use; or involvement in social activities beyond our time, energy and interest.

Evaluate your routines now and then to see whether some things consume more effort than they are worth — and at the expense of more important things.

Life is more than food, and the body more than clothing. (Luke 12:23)

Let my priorities be Your priorities, Father Almighty.

Prescription for Coping

The ability to laugh at ourselves can help us cope with problems and limitations.

Richard Wagner, the opera composer, was not able to play the piano well. When he was teased about his lack of ability, he would reply, "I play a good deal better than Berlioz." Composer Hector Berlioz didn't play the piano at all.

Franklin Roosevelt was paralyzed from the waist down as a result of polio. In speaking of his handicap, he once said, "I can't move around my office, but what advantage is there in moving around an office anyhow? I used to walk the rug in the old days, and what did I accomplish? I wore a hole in the rug."

Laughter is good medicine for stress or depression. But if you need stronger medical help, be willing to ask for it.

I will rejoice in the Lord, I will joy in the God of my salvation. (Habakkuk 3:18)

O, that I might always joy in You, God my Savior.

Running from Failure

Failure doesn't have to be fatal.

Englishman Roger Bannister became the first person in history to run the mile in under four minutes.

Yet his success originated in a failure in the 1952 Olympics. He was considered to be Great Britain's best distance runner, but failed to win any gold medals.

Because of that failure he decided to keep running rather than retire and devote all his attention to his medical studies. Two years later he ran his famous race.

He also completed his studies and became a physician.

Do not be afraid of failure. It's how you respond to failure that's important. It can be the beginning, not the end, if you don't let yourself give up.

Exhort one another . . . that none of you may be hardened by the deceitfulness of sin. (Hebrews 3:13)

That I might see failure as a beginning not an end, God my hope.

Early Emancipation Proclamation

Robert Carter III was one of the richest men in Virginia in the late 1700s. He owned 60,000 acres and more than five hundred slaves as his "absolute property."

But when about five hundred people gathered on July 28, 1991, near Montross, Virginia, it wasn't because of these facts. Instead, they were recalling his philosophy and generosity as shown in the document Carter filed August 1, 1791, in which he established a twenty-one-year schedule for freeing all his slaves.

Seventy years before President Abraham Lincoln's "Emancipation Proclamation," Carter wrote that he had become "convinced that to retain them in slavery is contrary to the true principles of Religion and Justice."

Individually, and as a nation, we are still struggling to eliminate every form of prejudice and injustice. Do your part, today, beginning with yourself.

Do not judge by appearances, but judge with right judgment. (John 7:24)

May we identify and eliminate our prejudices and biases, Just Judge.

Playing Ball for Love

The Baseball Hall of Fame in Cooperstown, New York, held a ceremony in the summer of 1991 honoring the many great players of the Negro League.

Many fans today don't recall the decades of segregated baseball. This was before Jackie Robinson, who had played with the Negro League's Kansas City Monarchs, broke the color-barrier with the Brooklyn Dodgers in 1947.

Life on the road was hard for the black players, especially since many hotels and restaurants would not accommodate them. They often played three games a day. And they played for love. One former Negro Leaguer, Preston Ingram, said, "You played for the fun of it. . . . I couldn't wait for summer to start. I'd rather bat than eat."

Such enthusiasm even in the face of injustice is worth remembering – and saluting. Enthusiasm adds zest to life, no matter how difficult things may be.

The righteous are bold as a lion. (Proverbs 28:1)

Embolden me, Redeemer, to live with joy and enthusiasm.

From the North Pole to California

On August 3, 1958, Seaman Denny Breese wrote to his brother Nick from aboard the submarine Nautilus. The letter marked the occasion of the nuclear-powered submarine's first voyage under the North Pole.

Thirty-two years later, the post office delivered it.

The present owners of the house asked around and learned that the father of the two brothers was still in the neighborhood. They brought him the letter.

Perhaps not surprisingly, the elder Mr. Breese hesitated to mail it to his son: "The odds of it getting lost again are ten million to one, but Nick might be out here soon, so maybe I could just wait and hand it to him."

When anything goes wrong, we tend to become cautious. That may not be bad if it leads to discretion and sound judgment. In other words, prudence.

Prudence is a virtue worth developing. Give it time.

May the Lord grant you discretion and understanding. (1 Chronicles 22:12)

Come, Holy Spirit, font of wisdom, come.

Promote Self-Respect

People often look for self-respect in the wrong places. They try to find it in power, in wealth, in fame.

Two generations ago, then Yale University president Whitney Griswold told graduates: "Self-respect cannot be hunted. It cannot be purchased. . . . It cannot be fabricated out of public relations. It comes to us . . . when we suddenly realize that knowing the good, we have done it; knowing the beautiful, we have served it; knowing the truth, we have spoken it."

To his observation, we might add: Self-respect comes to us when we recognize that we are all children of God, and we entrust ourselves to our Father's care.

Do not be afraid, little flock, for it is your Father's good pleasure to give you the kingdom. (Luke 12:32)

Father most holy, thank You for Your faithful covenant of love.

Traffic Tickets Save Lives

You might think that there's nothing in the world that would make you so grateful for three traffic tickets that you would actually thank the police officer. But Gloria Yzaguirre of Washington did just that.

Each $66 ticket was issued because two adults in the car were not wearing seat belts and a toddler was not fastened into a car seat. This incentive to start buckling up saved their lives two days later when the car was totaled in an accident.

"And I had to admit to (the police officer) that if he'd only given us a verbal warning, my daughter and I probably wouldn't be alive today."

So much in life is a matter of perspective. An upsetting annoyance becomes a blessing when it makes us do something that turns out to be good for us.

What do you need to see with a new point of view?

I reprove and discipline those whom I love. (Revelation 3:19)

Good Shepherd, help me accept Your way for my good — and Your glory.

Peace Prayer for Our World

There is a Children's Monument in Hiroshima's Peace Park to honor Sadako Sasaki and all the other children who were killed by the atomic bomb.

Sadako was two when the bomb hit, ten when she was diagnosed with leukemia and began her struggle to live. Before she died, Sadako, in her own appeal for peace, folded almost a thousand paper cranes because, in Japan, the crane is a symbol of life.

Her classmates, inspired by her courage, started a national campaign to honor her — and all other children like her. At the Children's Monument there is a place for the thousands of paper cranes that have been made by Japanese children in the cause of peace. And at the base of the Monument, there are these words:

"This is our cry, this is our prayer: Let there be peace in the world."

All of us should join in this cry, this prayer. Work and pray for peace in our world, our cities, our homes, ourselves.

Be at peace with one another. (Mark 9:50)

Lord of peace with justice, enable us to renounce the use of nuclear and biological weapons.

Vacation Values

Was your last vacation a near disaster? Maybe that's because you didn't work at it. A good vacation takes planning. Here are some ideas:

- Build some real leisure into your vacation — time to just loaf and relax.
- But avoid the extreme of sitting around doing nothing the whole time.
- See that everyone on vacation with you has time for themselves. Privacy is important.
- If there is work to be done, share it. That way everyone will have a good time.
- Allow time for parents to be away from the children.

By taking everyone's interests and concerns into account, your time away can be a time together and a genuine vacation from everyday routine. Be sure you don't take a vacation from thoughtfulness to one another and those you meet along the way.

Pursue love. (I Corinthians 14:1)

Teach me how to love, Jesus.

Brake that Fall into Anger

The elevator is not a modern invention. Lifts have been used in construction from the time the pyramids were built. But they were too dangerous for passengers. Cables could break – with disastrous results.

Then in 1854, Elisha Otis of Vermont found a way to make elevators safe. His invention used a large compressed spring. If the elevator cable went slack, this spring automatically snapped out, pushing two iron bars into notched guide rails in the elevator shaft. This locked the elevator in place, protecting passengers.

When tempers snap and anger gets out of control, the results can also be disastrous. We can't help feeling angry at times – anger is a normal emotion. But we can put a "safety lock" on what we say or do. Then, while keeping our anger in check, we can explore the cause of the anger and see what can be done about it.

Refrain from anger, and forsake wrath. Do not fret – it leads only to evil. (Psalm 37:8)

Help us keep our anger in check, patient Jesus who knew anger, but so often checked it.

Out of Darkest Depths – Light

It seems strange to us that deep-sea creatures can live in perpetual darkness. As light passes through the water, it is refracted and the colors of the spectrum are absorbed. First red disappears. At deeper levels, yellow, then green, and finally blue, leaving almost total darkness.

Most fish and other sea animals that live at depths below about a thousand feet make their own light. In some fish, light is produced by bacteria in certain parts of the body. Other fish have special cells that make light. To survive in the darkness, these deep-sea dwellers rely on the light produced within them.

Disaster can sometimes make our world seem as dark as the ocean depths. To get through life's dark times, we, too, must rely on the light from within us – the hope that comes from faith in God.

Teacher, do You not care that we are perishing? He woke up and rebuked the wind, and said to the sea, "Peace! Be still!" Then the wind ceased, and there was a dead calm. (Mark 4:38–39)

Jesus, grant us hope in You and faith in Your loving care.

By the Sea: A Banana Farm

La Conchita, a small California community nestled between the sea and 300-foot bluffs that rise behind the beach, is the site of the only banana farm in the continental United States.

By any standards, the twelve acre farm is small. But Doug Richardson, a former landscaper, and Paul Turner, care for 10,000 banana trees which produce up to 240 tons of bananas a year. That's about two-thirds of what the same amount of acreage might produce elsewhere but it's good enough for the owners.

Previously, Richardson had used banana plants in his yard as ground cover. Then he did some research and discovered that the climate in La Conchita was suitable for banana cultivation. There had never been a frost in the area that anyone could remember. During the summer growing season the temperature was an ideal 85 to 95 degrees. Nearby temperate ocean currents kept the area warm in winter.

Nature is remarkable for its variety. Learn about the weather, geography, plants and animals in your area. They echo the diversity of all creation and the wonder of our God who made them.

You cut openings for springs and torrents; you dried up ever-flowing streams. Yours is the . . . summer and winter. (Psalm 74:15–17)

In nature's diversity and fruitfulness, may I see Your diverse and fruitful unity, Triune God.

Building Confidence in Prayer

For too many, prayer is a problem. People want to know such things as "How am I to pray?" or "Why aren't my prayers answered?" or "How can I pray better?" or "Why do I feel unworthy when I pray?"

It would take books to answer such questions fully. But here are a few thoughts on prayer.

- Prayer builds on human weakness. God reminds us how much we need Him. A recovering alcoholic wrote, "Not until I turned my will and my life over to God's care did things change for me."
- Prayer promotes self-respect. There is something wrong with your prayer if you concentrate on your faults. Self-confidence comes when you begin to believe that God really does love you for yourself just as you are.
- Prayer rejoices in the presence of God. A woman wrote, "In my fifty-five years . . . I have found delight in the Lord for I always have Him beside me."
- Prayer is patient — *with God.* You can't plant an acorn one day and expect to sit in the oak tree's shade the next.

Pray daily. For your good. And God's delight!

I waited patiently for the Lord; He inclined to me and heard my cry. (Psalm 40:1)

Help me to pray, Holy Wisdom of God!

Of Sun, Summer and Flowers

What plant has been described as a true sun worshipper? . . . was grown in front of prairie pioneers' sod houses? . . . turns up in greengrocers' flower displays as well as in yards and vases? . . . been used to decorate everything from galvanized watering cans to museum quality dishes? . . .

Hint. Baseball players munch its dried seeds. Kansas has named it the state flower. And edible oil is pressed from its seeds.

Of course, it's the sunflower, that sometimes ragged, weedy, stunningly tall plant with the smiling, round, yellow heads.

If you think about it, sunflowers remind us of the infinite beauty of creation smiling even in August's shimmering heat and humidity.

"Come," my heart says, "seek His Face!" Your Face, Lord, do I seek. Do not hide Your Face from me. (Psalm 27:8)

Gracious God, thank You for the beauty of all creation, including myself.

Testing the Unknown

Many jobs entail risk, but one that seems almost synonymous with danger is that of test pilots. Their job is to check and evaluate the safety, operation and durability of an aircraft that's never been flown before.

They must be on guard at all times, and attentive to the slightest detail.

It's a demanding job that requires confidence and bravery because no matter how carefully test flights are planned, there is always the element of the unknown.

Truly, there is an element of risk and uncertainty in every new venture. Don't be afraid to step into the unknown simply because it is unknown. Progress always entails risk. Plan ahead intelligently and have courage.

All things are possible with God. (Mark 10:27)

Remind me, Redeemer, that indeed all things are possible with You at my side.

Children Still Need the "Other" Parent

When a married couple breaks up, it's always a pain-filled experience. Unfortunately, while they are consumed by their own practical and emotional problems, they often forget that separation can be even harder on children.

A Midwestern judge offers sobering words for these mothers and fathers: "No matter what you think of the other party . . . these children are one half of each of you. Remember that, because every time you tell your child what an 'idiot' his father is, or what a 'fool' his mother is . . . you are telling the child that half of him is bad.

"That is not love. That is possession. Think more about your children and less about yourselves, and make yours a selfless kind of love, not foolish or selfish, or your children will suffer."

However hard your life may be, put your children first. The tougher the times, the more they need you both.

The righteous walk in integrity – happy are the children who follow them! (Proverbs 20:7)

Help married couples respect each other and their children, Abba.

A Life-Changing Truth

Henri Nouwen, the renowned author, told this story about his first meeting with the late Mother Teresa of Calcutta a number of years ago.

He spent a good ten minutes telling her about his problems and how difficult and complicated his life was. He asked her advice. She said, "When you spend one hour a day adoring our Lord and never do anything that you know is wrong . . . you will be fine!"

According to Father Nouwen, "Her words became engraved on my heart and mind because their directness and simplicity cut to the center of my problems. Her answer came from God's place, not from the place of my complaints. She had, I knew, spoken the truth. I, on the other hand, had the rest of my life to live it."

The way to a life well-lived is prayer and good deeds.

There may come a time when recovery lies in the hands of physicians, for they too pray to the Lord that he grant them success in diagnosis and in healing, for the sake of preserving life. (Sirach 38:13–14)

God, teach me Your wisdom.

Ben Franklin, Swimming Instructor

In addition to his other accomplishments, Benjamin Franklin was adept at swimming. He developed a method to teach yourself to swim.

It calls for walking into water until the water reaches your chest, then turning and dropping an egg in front of you and diving for it. You would be moving toward shallow water, so there would be no reason to fear.

In diving, he said you would learn that your body would buoy you up. Additionally, in trying to reach the egg, you would learn to propel yourself through the water.

Sounds like a simple idea. Perhaps it even works.

Remember that knowledge, after all, is for sharing. Learn, not only for your own sake, but for those you can teach.

God . . . desires everyone to be saved and to come to the knowledge of the truth. (I Timothy 2:3–4)

Send us Your Holy Spirit, Jesus!

From Clothes to Trash and Back Again

Ranya Kelly needed a box to ship some things. So she checked the trash bins behind a local mall. What she found was five hundred pairs of shoes.

Mrs. Kelly gathered the unused, discarded shoes and brought them to a shelter. That's how she began her now decade-long commitment: get unsold clothing to people who haven't the means to buy them. At first stores were reluctant to help. "They were afraid people would try to return donated items for refunds," says the Arvada, Colorado, homemaker.

But now, a number of companies regularly supply shoes, clothing, blankets and towels. From their basement redistribution center Ranya Kelly, her husband Byron and other volunteers send out over $2 million worth of donated merchandise. Shelters, hospitals, church groups and other agencies get the items to those who most need them.

You never know when some small event will change your life and the lives of others for the better – if you turn it into an opportunity to do good.

Share your bread with the hungry, and bring the homeless poor into your house; when you see the naked . . . cover them. (Isaiah 58:7)

Lord, let me be a useful tool of Your peace and comfort to anyone bruised by life.

Picture Imperfect

A Zen priest was in charge of a small temple famous for its beautiful garden. He tried to have a perfect garden. One day when he was expecting guests, he spent the entire morning raking up all the fallen leaves and removing them. He sprinkled and even combed some of the moss to make it perfect.

When he had finished, he turned to an old master from a nearby temple, who had been watching him work, and asked, "Isn't it beautiful? Don't you think the garden now looks just the way it should?" "Yes, your garden is beautiful," said the master, "but something is missing."

The old man walked to the center of the garden where a tree was growing. He shook the tree, and since it was autumn, leaves scattered over the garden. "That's what it needed," said the master.

Perfection is an ideal, an elusive state. It doesn't exist in real gardens or real life. Problems and disappointments are as inevitable as autumn's falling leaves. See them as a means of growth, a natural part of life.

"Love your enemies, and pray for those who persecute you, so that you may be children of your Father in heaven." (Matthew 5:43–45)

Enable me, God, to cooperate with Your grace as I strive to relax into all You created me to be.

Good Porches, Good Neighbors

"This world would be a better place if everyone had a front porch," says William Martin of Northport, New York.

The trend today is to build houses with a backyard and patio instead of the front porch that was popular years ago. True, a patio at the back of the house affords more privacy — maybe too much privacy.

Martin thought something important was lost, so, a few years ago, he added a porch, and now calls it "one of the best moves we ever made."

The old-fashioned front porch was more than just a place to sit and relax, to enjoy the outdoors protected from sun and rain. It was a place that encouraged friendliness with neighbors. People walking by would smile and wave, often stopping to talk.

People need one another. Even the simple warmth of a friendly greeting can help lift our spirits.

Better is a neighbor who is nearby than kindred who are far away. (Proverbs 27:10)

Help us be good neighbors, Jesus of Nazareth.

Everybody's Doing It

Some years ago, a school superintendent in Arkansas noticed that a junior high school girl was wearing one red sock and one blue sock. He asked her if this had some special meaning.

The teenager explained that she was wearing different socks because she was an individualist. She said, "I have a right to be different if I want to – besides, all the kids are doing it."

Fads in clothing have long been a way for teenagers to assert their independence from parents and gain acceptance by peers.

Conforming to peer pressure in the way they dress is usually harmless. But teens are often pressured to do dangerous things such as drinking or using drugs. Parents can help teens resist harmful peer pressure by building up their confidence and teaching them what individuality really is.

[Clothe] yourselves with the new self, which is being renewed in knowledge after the image of its Creator. (Colossians 3:10)

Youth from Nazareth, inspire teens to follow Your ways, not dangerous fads.

Clean Humor

Comedienne Jennifer Rawlings was disturbed by vulgar jokes and coarse language she heard other comedians using in clubs. And she was embarrassed when her whole family came to see her perform and heard the vulgar barrage, too. It inspired her to create evenings of clean adult comedy, called "Take Out the Trash."

The events, produced and hosted by Rawlings, play to crowds in comedy clubs, churches and other venues throughout Southern California. Entire families can enjoy comedians who get big laughs with clean material.

Rawlings still plays the regular comedy clubs, so that audiences can hear an alternative to raunchy humor. "I've never prayed for a laugh," she says. "But I have prayed to God that my performance will be positive and that I'll have a good influence on people."

That sounds like a wonderfully appropriate prayer for each of us as we start our day's work.

This is the Lord for whom we have waited; let us be glad and rejoice in His salvation. (Isaiah 25:9)

Thanks for the joy of Your Presence, Jesus.

Philanthropy of Compassion

A former Christopher staff member, Charles Ascenzi, now deceased, was an unusually kind, nonjudgmental person.

Another staff member was with Charles one day when he was approached by a shabby street person. The man told a wildly improbable tale of woe, but Charles gave him $10.

After the panhandler left, the other staff member said to Charles, "You shouldn't have given that man money. The story he told couldn't have been true. He just made it up."

"Yes," said Charles, "but imagine how it would feel to be so desperate you had to make up a story like that."

Instead of judging the man, he chose to show compassion for his need.

With the judgment you pronounce you will be judged. (Matthew 7:2)

Teach me to be kind and nonjudgmental, Jesus.

Time for "Thank you"

A while back blue skies and a bright sun didn't make Californians happy. They were cause for gloom. In the drought-parched state, residents were so depressed by brown lawns that they had dead grass painted green. To them a "good" day was a cloudy day. Weather forecasters spoke of the "hope of rain" or the "promise of snow."

We take rain or snow for granted, even complain about it, until drought reminds us what a great blessing it is.

It's also easy to take for granted the people in our lives. We forget what a blessing their help and moral support provide.

Let others know that you appreciate them. Take time to say "Thank you."

While you're at it, stop to say "Thank You" to God as well.

Bless the Lord, all rain and dew; sing praise to Him. (Daniel 3:42)

Thank You, God, for rain, dew, frost, and snow; for bubbling springs and all water.

Taming Malignant Elements

"Confucius taught that it is better to change a malignant element into a useful one, rather than kill it," says Doctor Wang Zhenyi. Doctor Zhenyi, a Chinese cancer researcher, and Doctor Laurent Degos, a French blood specialist, applied this principle to their research. Their goal: a cure for a severe form of leukemia.

The usual treatment for leukemia is to kill the cancerous cells before their uncontrolled growth kills the patient.

Doctors Zhenyi and Degos instead used a derivative of Vitamin A to tame the cancerous cells so they would grow in the controlled fashion of healthy cells.

As a reward they shared a $100,000 Charles F. Kettering Prize from the General Motors Cancer Foundation and each received a gold medal.

We all have malignant elements in our personality, uncontrolled anger, for example. Learn to tame them. Then all that energy can go into a good cause.

Your anger does not produce God's righteousness. (James 1:20)

Lessen my burden of anger, Lord.

Honest Family Returns Cash

Two children, Daniel and Patrick Rein, found an envelope on the sidewalk near their home. They saw that it contained a lot of money and took it to their father to see what should be done with it.

The envelope held $2,200 in cash and some college forms, but there was no name on the forms. Mr. Rein knew that the money must belong to a student, probably someone who had worked and saved to pay tuition. He immediately phoned a nearby college.

The money turned out to be the life savings of seventeen-year-old José Rodriguez. He had dropped the envelope on the way to pay his tuition. Thanks to the honesty of the Rein family, he was able to attend college as he had planned.

Honesty is one way we show our concern for other people.

Birds roost with their kind; so honesty comes home to those who practice it. (Sirach 27:9)

May honesty be in my heart and home, Savior.

Dressed for Genuine Success

Meet a teenager who calls herself a recovering junkie. She says she was hooked on designer clothes!

Expensive clothes made her feel important, so she spent much of her time and money on them. She didn't realize that clothing could become a habit until she learned that a friend resorted to shoplifting to get his many designer clothes.

She broke her habit by switching to inexpensive clothing and then using the money she had saved to treat herself to Broadway shows and art museums.

Now she has real interests and doesn't need what she calls "make-believe self-importance." She says, "I no longer look the part, because I'm too busy living it."

This young woman recognized a destructive habit and took steps to free herself from it. Is there anything we depend on more than is good for us?

For freedom Christ has set us free.
(Galatians 5:1)

Liberator, free us from our bad habits.

Faith Renewed

Ann Cleland of Des Moines, Iowa, found her life turned upside down by the devastating floods that hit the Midwest in 1993. The waters broke right after she moved into a new home and renovated her beauty salon.

Her home and business were ruined. Her teenage daughter dealt with serious grief and depression. Ann spent days working at a local beauty parlor and nights rebuilding her salon.

She felt lonely and helpless. But she found kindness in friends and strangers alike. Volunteers from her church helped clean her house. People in Connecticut sent her $500. A man redesigned her salon at little cost and volunteers fixed her plumbing and wiring for free. Ann Cleland was amazed at how helpful people were to each other. She said, "Month after month of God's compassionate provision changed my fear to renewed faith."

Try to bring some of God's love to someone you know who needs a helping hand. You will be expressing God's own compassion.

Stretch out Your hand from on high; set me free and rescue me from the mighty waters.
(Psalm 144:7)

There are so many "mighty waters" in my life, Lord. Rescue me. Keep me safe.

Score One for Determination

The record for most persistent golfer may have been set back in 1912 at the ladies' invitational at Shawnee-on-Delaware, Pennsylvania.

In the qualifying round, a woman took 166 strokes to make the 130-yard sixteenth hole.

Her tee shot went into the river and the ball floated downstream. She and her husband jumped into a rowboat and set out after the ball. They followed it a mile and a half before she was able to beach it. Then she had to play through the woods all the way back to the golf course.

This golfer's score may have been poor, but her determination was truly remarkable.

When we do poorly at something we undertake, it's important not to become discouraged and give up. We can learn from our failure and do better the next time.

Hear the word, hold it fast in an honest and good heart, and bear fruit with patient endurance. (Luke 8:15)

Give us Your patience, God.

Paving the Way to Heaven

"Get dirty for God. Go lay a brick!"

This is the slogan of a summer mission program — a program in which teens help with projects like building hospitals and orphanages in developing countries.

But it's good advice for all of us, wherever we are, whatever we do.

If you think there's nothing you can do to help on some worthwhile project, you're wrong. There's always behind-the-scenes work. This "dirty work" may not be glamorous, but it's important. Like buildings, successful projects are constructed bit by bit, from many small components.

Do one thing today. One letter, one phone call, one act of kindness — there are many ways to lay a brick for God.

Do you not remember the five loaves for the five thousand, and how many baskets you gathered? (Matthew 16:9)

How may I do some one little thing for You, my God?

Common Philosophy

Seven people chosen at random were asked, "What is the philosophy that guides your life?" Here are their answers:

- I just try to do my best.
- Slow down and enjoy the little things.
- Don't get in a rut.
- Take time to do what you would like to do.
- Relax and look at life in perspective.
- Take things a day at a time.
- See that your life has variety.

Taken together, these people seem to be saying that to enjoy life to the fullest it helps to be a well-rounded person with many different interests. Give yourself a chance to develop in new ways, in new interests. You owe it to yourself. To others. And to God, your Maker.

Better is a handful with quietness than two handfuls with toil. (Ecclesiastes 4:6)

Slow me down, Lord, that I may develop as the human person You made me.

It's a Stretch

Ever wonder how some time-honored traditions got started?

Next time you're at a baseball game here's one you can share with your neighbors during the seventh inning stretch.

Brother Jasper Brennan was the athletic director and baseball coach of Manhattan College in the 1880s. He was also the prefect of discipline. When students attended ball games they had to sit quietly or Brother Jasper would take them to task.

But he noticed that the student spectators were especially fidgety at one game. So he told them to stand and stretch. It became a regular event. And when the team played an exhibition game with the New York Giants, the popularity of the seventh inning stretch spread.

Some ideas catch on quickly. Others don't make it to first base. To give your ideas a chance keep on slugging.

Let us hold fast to the confession of our hope without wavering. (Hebrews 10:23)

Let every one of my hopes and dreams be a small reflection of my hope in You, Divine Friend.

Education – a Lifelong Companion

The English essayist Joseph Addison once described education as the "companion which no misfortune can depress, no crime can destroy, no enemy can alienate, no despotism can enslave. At home, education is a friend, abroad it is an introduction. In solitude, education is a solace, and in society it is an ornament. It chastens vice," he continued, and "it guides virtue."

"Without it," Addison asked, "what is man but a splendid slave, a reasoning savage?"

The interesting thing about education is that it's the one thing we are willing to pay for and not get. Many young people find it hard to concentrate on their schoolwork. Encouragement and a good example help.

Real education, however, doesn't end with a graduation. That's only a beginning. Learning is meant to be part of a person's whole life.

Be filled with . . . wisdom and understanding. (Colossians 1:9)

Come, source of all our wisdom, Holy Spirit, come.

Miracle: A Second Life

Wendy Marsh wrote to The Christophers a while back to tell us how an organ transplant changed her life.

When polycystic kidney disease was diagnosed in this mother of five from Amarillo, Texas, her "kidneys were functioning at less than fifteen percent normal output."

In the weeks after the transplant operation, Mrs. Marsh's body started to reject the kidney. She became allergic to medicine. Pain and hallucinations followed.

But there was help. "The power of prayers came to cure me as I lay in the ugly green hospital room," says the former patient.

In the years since then, she has come to appreciate "the miracle of a second life," and hopes "more people will sign organ donor cards so that others may be blessed with life-giving miracles."

That's a very good idea from someone who is living "a second life."

Jesus said . . . "I am the gate for the sheep . . . I came that they may have life, and have it abundantly." (John 10:7, 10)

Grant me the holy desire, Merciful Savior, to protect all life at every stage.

Rules for Respect

Jesus said that we are to love our neighbors as we love ourselves. Here are some suggestions for showing that love for others and for ourselves:

- Make your own decisions about your life.
- Live by your set of moral values. Let this be your guide to relationships.
- Accept responsibility for solving your own problems.
- Do not accept inappropriate behavior from others. Voice your objections. Leave situations rather than let yourself be mistreated.
- Allow others to do for themselves, to make their own mistakes and to learn from them.
- Treat yourself and others with gentleness. Appreciate your own worth and that of your neighbor.

Bear in mind that only to the extent that you love and respect yourself will you be able to love others and God.

Love your neighbor as yourself. (Matthew 19:19)

God, help me to value my life and that of all Your children.

A Boss's Kindness

A Texas woman received a lasting gift from her boss.

After working five years to put her husband through school, she wanted to take his graduation day off so the family could celebrate. Her boss reminded her that it would be one of their busiest days of the year. He would only allow her enough time to go to the ceremony, then he wanted her back on the job.

The worker told him that wasn't enough. The day meant a lot to her family. The atmosphere at work grew strained over the next few weeks as she ignored her supervisor or treated him curtly. Finally, he called her into his office. The woman was sure she would be fired. Instead, he said, "I don't want anger and bitterness between us. You may have the day off."

Later, when that employee became a supervisor, she remembered the lesson that sometimes kindness is more important than being right. Even more so if you're the boss.

The fruit of the Spirit is love, joy, peace, patience, kindness. (Galatians 5:22)

Enable us to imitate Your kindness to us, Spirit of God.

Some Innovations Pay Off

If you ever look at a new item on the market and say, "Now, why didn't I think of that?" you have lots of company. Some things seem so obvious — after an inventor comes up with them.

Back in 1905 Frank Epperson accidentally froze a glass of lemonade with a stirrer in it. But, it wasn't until eighteen years later that he patented "frozen fruit water on a stick," also known as the Popsicle.

Epperson also came up with Popsicle's famous "twin-stick." During the Great Depression he realized that customers had to feel they were really getting their money's worth. With the second stick, two snack eaters could be happy for the price of one.

So if you have a flair for creativity or if you'd like to develop one, let your mind toy with different ideas. Exercise your capacity for discovery. You never know until you try.

Be rich in good works, generous, and ready to share. (I Timothy 6:18)

Show us how to use the skills You've given us to make life more humane, Creator.

Peace and All Good

Everyone who drives has had bad days on the road — cut off by other drivers, drivers who are too slow or too fast, or just rude or unthinking. But how often do we take time to show compassion and respect for our fellow drivers?

One Long Island woman tries each day.

Mary Lou Berton of East Islip, New York, has a license plate bearing the words, "Pax et Bonum." She explained, "Francis of Assisi, Man of Peace, greeted everyone this way — peace and good — and so I greet my fellow travelers along the way."

Making the effort to share kindness and courtesy with strangers can make us all feel good. It might even get somebody else thinking about trying to do the same.

Pax et Bonum! Peace and Good!

Greet one another with a kiss.
(I Corinthians 16:20)

Inspire us to deeds of kindness, God. Let me take the lead and not wait for others to be nice to me first.

How to Make a Wise Decision

Change is not always easy, but a life without change has its drawbacks too. Sometimes life forces a change on us for which we may feel unprepared, but most of the time we have the opportunity to think through a change; to make a decision.

Many people make what they call a Benjamin Franklin or pro and con list.

On a piece of paper, write at the top the potential change or the decision which needs to be made. Below that make two columns. Label one "pro" — the positive reasons for deciding in favor of the change; the other, "con" — the reasons against the change. Assign numerical values, say one to five, to each item, so the unimportant items don't outweigh what is truly important.

Ponder what you've written.

Share your ideas with a friend or two. Let them add their ideas. Ask yourself if are there more pros or more cons to be added to the list. After reflecting and maybe putting the list away for awhile, add up the columns.

Pray. Trust in God. Make your decision. Then, if needed, take action.

As He who called you is holy, be holy yourselves in all your conduct. (1 Peter 1:15)

May the deepest change in my life, God, be movement toward a truly whole and holy life.

Disaster at Sea

One of the most tragic disasters in American maritime history was the burning of the luxury liner Morro Castle in the Atlantic in September, 1934. More than 130 people lost their lives.

The toll could have been much worse because it was first reported that all hands had been saved. Despite that report, John and Jim Bogan, captains of a New Jersey party fishing boat, assembled a crew at 3:30 in the morning.

"We are going to be needed," John Bogan argued. "We'll be able to help somebody out there." He was right. For seven hours they were on the scene plucking survivors out of the stormy seas.

People near and far need aid and comfort. Follow your instinct to lend a hand. Not a day passes that your mercy is not vital in this world.

Let us then with confidence draw near to . . . receive mercy and find grace. (Hebrews 4:16)

Make me confident of Your mercy and grace, God my help.

Growth in Adversity

Bonsai, or dwarf potted trees, have long been admired in Japan. Today, most of them are dwarfed artificially, but originally they were trees naturally stunted by adverse conditions.

Japanese collectors searched for dwarf trees struggling to survive on rocky cliffs or barren slopes. There a tree might grow only a few feet high instead of the hundred feet or so it could have reached under better conditions.

These tenacious survivors can be more beautiful than their kin that grow in sheltered gardens and fertile soil. Their gnarled limbs have strength and character.

We, too, have greater strength than we may realize. History is filled with accounts of people who have survived handicaps and hardships, and who grew in the beauty of wisdom and compassion.

I have refined you . . . I have tested you in the furnace of adversity. (Isaiah 48:10)

Jesus, teach us to be courageous and compassionate.

Break Barriers to Listening

Humorist Ambrose Bierce defined a bore as "a person who talks when you wish him to listen."

Do you want to be a better listener? Then become aware of you personal barriers to listening.

Perhaps you don't like what you're hearing so you "tune out." You may even think you already know what the other person is going to say. Again, you don't bother to listen.

Some words, phrases or subjects may make you defensive or uncomfortable. Does the speaker annoy you? Or have poor delivery?

Awareness of potential problems as a listener is the beginning of better listening. And genuine communication. Admit your limitations and be willing to learn.

They were astonished at his teaching, for [Jesus] taught them as one having authority. (Mark 1:22)

Open my ears, Jesus, to all the nuances of Your words.

Monday, Monday

Psychologists are finding that there is some truth in the saying, "Blue Monday."

But don't be discouraged. Here are some ideas for coping with the Monday morning blahs.

- Start with preventive medicine. Over-indulgence of any kind over the weekend – especially Sunday night – will add to your difficulties on Monday morning.
- On Friday, put aside until Monday some pleasant work that you like to do. It will give you something to look forward to.
- Offer all the little things necessary to get going in the morning as a prayer.

There are ways to beat the blues. It just takes a little planning. Every day is worth a special effort to get the most out of it, including enjoyment.

This is the day which the Lord has made; let us rejoice and be glad in it. (Psalm 118:24)

When I have the blahs, Jesus, remind me that the day is Your present to me, to do with what I will.

Success Depends on Hard Work

Today, machines enable us to do jobs from calculations to laundry at the push of a button. But it's a mistake to expect instant, push-button results in everything we do. Most enterprises and achievements grow slowly, often from small beginnings and with many failures, and nearly always through hard work.

Luther Burbank, so successful at plant breeding that he was known as the wizard of horticulture, once commented: "To find this luscious strawberry, I grew 500,000 new plants – and then made a bonfire with 499,999 of them."

The Burbank potato also resulted from years of patient work. In one experiment he planted and grew twenty-three varieties. Of these, twenty-two were failures. The twenty-third was the famous potato later named in his honor.

If we find ourselves becoming discouraged, it may help to remember that success is rarely easy. Achievements of any kind are likely to be built on foundations of patience and hard work and failures.

You need endurance, so that when you have done the will of God, you may receive what was promised. (Hebrews 10:36)

In difficulties, in trials and in discouragement, God grant me enduring patience and hope.

"Once in a Blue Moon"

If you ever wondered just how often "once in a blue moon" is, here's the answer: it happens about every thirty-two months.

A blue moon is the term for the second full moon in a given month. Since a full moon occurs every twenty-nine and a half days, a blue moon is possible in every month except February.

And, yes, when the weather conditions are just right, the moon really can look bluish.

Check an almanac or the weather page of your local newspaper to find out when the next one occurs. Then look up at the night sky. When you do look to the heavens there's a universe of wonder and beauty God has given us to appreciate.

Take a moment today to notice, to enjoy, and to say "thanks."

It is the moon that marks the changing seasons. . . . From the moon comes the sign for festal days, a light that wanes when it completes its course. The new moon . . . renews itself; how marvelous is it in this change, a beacon to the hosts on high, shining in the vault of the heavens! (Sirach 43:6, 7–8)

How beautiful the moon in its phases, how gentle its blue-white light, Creator, who set such beauty in the vastness of space.

Encourage! Encourage! Encourage!

Have you ever been in the position of wanting to offer a word of encouragement to somebody who seemed to need it, but let the opportunity slip by?

You're not alone. And that's too bad. An encouraging remark can make someone's day. Occasionally it can even change a life — and a world.

Dr. Dale Turner tells how Alexander Graham Bell described his theory of telegraphing speech to the director of the Smithsonian Institute. Bell concluded by confessing that he didn't have enough knowledge of electricity to develop and test his theory.

His enthusiastic colleague urged him, "Well then, get it!" Bell did. And we, in time, got the benefit of his inventive genius with the development of the telephone.

So, next time, don't hesitate, speak up. In large ways or small, your encouragement matters.

Consider how to provoke one another to love and good deeds . . . encouraging one another.
(Hebrews 10:24–25)

Holy Spirit, show me how to "provoke" and encourage others to goodness!

Fun for Fundraising

Efforts to address any social need require money and plenty of it. And one of the greatest needs is feeding the homebound elderly.

Recently, a fundraiser let participants play a shortened game of Monopoly for real money and fun. Proceeds went to Citymeals-on-Wheels, an agency which feeds the homebound elderly.

Others watched for a fee of $75. And they were asked to buy a block to feed "all the homebound elderly on a particular block on weekends and holidays for a year." It was one innovative way to raise funds for a good cause, and entertain folks as well.

What creative idea can you think of to raise money for a good cause while having fun at the same time? Put your talents to work to do something to benefit others.

Oppressing the poor in order to enrich oneself . . . will lead only to loss. (Proverbs 22:16)

Make me creative and generous with time and talents, not only with money, Savior

One Creative Manager

For a supervisor or employer, group leader or coach, bringing out the best in others is important to the success of the individual and the team. It requires understanding people. As Joe McCarthy, manager of the New York Yankees during the thirties and forties demonstrated, it also calls for creativity.

One day, he approached his shortstop Frank Crosetti, saying, "I'm not satisfied with the way Lou Gehrig is playing first base. He is too lackadaisical. I want you to help me. From now on, charge every ball. When you get it, fire it as quickly and as hard as you can to first base. . . . Throw it fast and make it tough for him."

Later, a coach commented to McCarthy, "I guess you were trying to wake up Gehrig." The manager responded, "There wasn't a thing wrong with Gehrig. Crosetti was the one who was sleeping. I wanted to wake up Crosetti."

**"Keep awake – for you do not know when the master of the house will come, in the evening, or at midnight, or at cockcrow, or at dawn, or else he may find you asleep when he comes suddenly."
(Mark 13:35–36)**

Help me be alert to the signs of the times, Merciful Savior, and to signs of my own apathy.

Freedom of Religion: The First Step

The First Amendment to the Constitution of the United States of America, with its clause prohibiting the establishment of an official religion or interfering with the free exercise of religion, is generally considered the foundation for the nation's religious liberty.

Yet, the amendment, a part of the Bill of Rights, has an antecedent in Article VI of the Constitution. Article VI provides that "No religious test shall ever be required as a qualification to any office or public trust under the United States." Charles Pinckney of South Carolina, who was to serve as both governor of his state and member of the U. S. Senate, prepared this "religious test" article and pushed for its inclusion in the Constitution adopted in Philadelphia, September 17, 1787.

This was no small thing. Most states barred Catholics, Jews and Quakers from political office and there was little political profit in arguing to the contrary.

As citizens, we should encourage today's political leaders to be just as willing to push for what is right, even when it is unpopular. Then we have to back them up.

You shall not render an unjust judgment . . . with justice you shall judge your neighbor. (Leviticus 19:15)

Help me take a stand for justice and for those who pursue it, God.

Basic Balancing Act

Scientists tell us that walking is a process of falling forward.

When we are standing still, our bodies are balanced. But in order to walk, we have to upset the balance.

First, we relax the calf muscles, which makes us fall forward. To break the fall, we throw one leg forward. The body is again balanced temporarily, until the other leg pushes forward. Then the body again lurches forward, and that leg breaks the fall. We walk by repeatedly losing and then regaining our balance.

To move forward in the things we do, we also have to take risks and upset the comfortable status quo.

Like a child learning to walk, we will probably have some falls in the process. But we learn by picking ourselves up and trying again.

It was I who taught Ephraim to walk. (Hosea 11:3)

Teach me anew to walk in Your way, God of the Covenant.

Quality Is Made of Details

What is the difference between a superb violin produced by a master like Antonio Stradivari and a mediocre one by a less gifted artisan? *Details.*

There are virtually no items in the making of a violin that do not affect its sound. Different woods are used for the back and belly, supporting ribs, linings, blocks, and other parts. The fiber and density of each type of wood affects the pitch and tone.

Because the thickness of the wood has a marked effect on the tone, it is crucial to cut and shape according to the quality and curvature of the wood. The size of blocks and the shape of sound holes also affect the violin's tone.

Even the quality of the varnish is important to the production of a full, rich sound. Stradivari had his own varnish recipe, which has never been duplicated.

In life as in violin making, details make the difference and enhance the quality of our lives. A smile and "hello" can make a stranger feel welcome. A word of praise can give new incentive to someone who's discouraged.

If I speak in the tongues of mortals and of angels but have not love, I am a noisy gong or a clanging cymbal. (I Corinthians 13:1)

Point out to me, Lord, how the "small things" of daily life can be expressions of charity.

Tender, Loving Care for Planet Earth

For years, scientists watched one of the peaks in Vermont's Green Mountain range. They were concerned about what at first appeared to be an unexplained decay.

This beautiful patch of forest was deteriorating rapidly. Evergreens lost their needles. Once-majestic red spruce trees began dying. The mountain took on a barren, desolate look.

Scientists investigated every possible natural cause of this collapse. They considered drought, disease, and insect attack. Finally, they found that the culprit was air pollution.

It is easy to blame industry, government or other people and to expect them to solve the problem. However, all of us have to do our part to halt and reverse the damage pollution inflicts on our earth, our home. Become ecology-minded. Become an active participant in protecting our planet Earth.

This is the only home we have.

The heavens are the Lord's heaven, but the earth He has given to human beings. (Psalm 115:16)

May we treat Your gift of the earth, our home, with the love it and You deserve, Creator-God.

Breaking Down Walls of Prejudice

It has been said that "every bigot was once a child free of prejudice." In other words, prejudice is learned. But respect and tolerance are learned as well. Here are some steps parents and other adults can take:

- Teach that differences are normal.
- Remind children to see each human being as a unique child of God.
- Encourage youngsters to see the good in every person and in every group.
- Stress what we have in common, especially our common humanity.
- Don't generalize from isolated incidents or use stereotypes.
- When you are confronted by prejudice, speak up.
- Educate yourself and youngsters about the history and cultures of other people of the world.

Charlotte Bronte wrote, "Prejudices . . . are most difficult to eradicate from the heart whose soil has never been loosened or fertilized by education."

Lessons in tolerance or prejudice will be learned. For better or worse.

The compassion of human beings is for their neighbors, but the compassion of the Lord is for every living thing. (Sirach 18:13)

Teach me, instruct me, form me, Father, that in turn I may teach, instruct and form others by the example of my life.

Good Sports

In children's sports, pediatricians say, winning at any cost means losing. When children are under too much pressure to win, they are more likely to suffer physical injuries and emotional stress. They can come to dread sports, too.

Health professionals remind parents that the purpose of sports for young people is not to train star athletes, but for children to play and have fun, and to develop social and motor skills.

Helping children develop self-confidence, a sense of fair play, and the ability to work together contributes to true and lasting success in sports as well as in life.

Encourage children to put the *play* back in "Play ball!"

Live as children of light — for the fruit of the light is found in all that is good and right and true. (Ephesians 5:8–9)

Guide parents as they raise their children, Holy Spirit.

In the Mood for Music

Muzak has been described as music "to be heard but not listened to," bland "wallpaper" music we but don't pay much attention to in elevators, offices and stores.

Yet according to a Muzak Company executive, the unobtrusive sound is carefully programmed to affect the listener's mood. They use very low-key music with which listeners feel comfortable. Amplified guitars, loud drums, and tubas are avoided.

Music is divided into fifteen-minute segments played in a carefully planned sequence throughout the day. Segments played from 10 to 11a.m. and 3 to 4 p.m., for example, are stimulating, since workers are likely to be tired. Soothing music is played after 12 noon to counter lunchtime excitement as well as after 6 p.m.

If such music's influence is harmless, perhaps even beneficial, other forms may not be. Whether listening to commercials, news or entertainment programs on radio or television, reading magazines, newspapers or books, or browsing the internet, exercise your critical judgement. Teach yourself to make up your own mind.

**The ear tests words as the palate tastes food.
(Job 34:3)**

Show me how to be an alert and discriminating listener and reader, Creator, who formed my ears and eyes and mind.

Sanctuary from Stress – and Much More

Rabbi Abraham Joshua Heschel called the Sabbath "a sanctuary in time."

In an age when we rush to cram as much activity as possible into every minute, it's especially important to take and make a time of refuge from constant doing, to have a time for being. A Sabbath rest gives us time to spend on our relationship with our family and friends, and our God. It gives us time for ourselves.

The sanctuary of the Sabbath is the day on which we allow ourselves to accomplish nothing, to achieve nothing, to waste time. It is a day for silence and music, conversation, and reading, walking slowly and playing games and especially for prayer and meditation.

A day of "sanctuary" gives us rest emotionally as well as physically; frees us from preoccupations that separate us from God's healing presence; renews us with the peace that only God can give; prevents stress from damaging our spiritual, emotional, and physical health; and gives us a taste of the eternal rest promised to us.

Ought not this woman, a daughter of Abraham whom Satan bound for eighteen long years, be set free from this bondage on the Sabbath day? (Luke 13:16)

Liberate me, Lord of the Sabbath, so that I can enter into Your rest even here and now.

Have You Heard?

Even scrupulously honest people can unwittingly spread false information. At some time or other, most of us have repeated a rumor that proved to be untrue. And even true stories easily become so distorted that they have little relation to fact.

Psychologists have identified common ways stories change as they pass from person to person: incidents may be exaggerated to make a more dramatic story; details may be forgotten, or what people hear may be influenced by their prejudices.

Rumors can damage businesses, ruin reputations, ignite racial and religious tensions — at the very least cause needless anxiety.

When you hear a story, ask yourself, "What's the source of this story?" and, "Is there any real evidence to support it?" Don't unthinkingly pass on rumors that could do harm.

Take responsibility for your words.

Rumor follows rumor. (Ezekiel 7:26)

Lord, make my speech charitable, honest, wise, and joy-filled.

"Be Kind, Be Kind, Be Kind . . . "

Kindness comes from an Old English word for family. It is *within* the family that we learn kindness, help for those in need, and a thoughtful attitude.

And it is *from* the family that we carry kindness —a thoughtful attitude and a desire to help the needy to our jobs, our community, our fellow worshippers, strangers.

Not that kindness is easy. It isn't always simple for either the giver or the receiver and it can even become a burden. But it is always humane and humanizing.

Jesus taught the need for kindness when He told the parable of the Good Samaritan and his praiseworthy deed of kindness on that desolate desert road down to Jericho from Jerusalem.

As Jan van Ruysbroeck, a medieval Rhenish mystic, wrote, "Be kind, be kind, be kind, and you will soon be saints."

Let's be kind.

Pleasant words are like a honeycomb, sweetness to the soul and health to the body. (Proverbs 16:24)

Help me be kind to myself; my speech and actions towards others gracious, strong yet gentle Jesus.

Flowers and Prayers

A South Dakota farmer found time for God by watching the sunflowers.

The year Brian Barber planted sunflowers, he thought his crop was doomed by alternating periods of rain and drought. As the earth cracked, he noticed that the sunflowers grew roots that wandered this way and that until they found a crack in the soil.

Barber wanted to give more time to God. But as a farmer he was either always busy or bone tired. Until he learned to look for the cracks. In his case he began while farming to meditate on the Biblical parables that have to do with working the land.

As a result, he said, he developed a connection with the Biblical farmers and with the God who made the harvest bountiful.

You can incorporate more prayer into your own life, if you let your imagination guide you.

He spent the night in prayer. (Luke 6:12)

Lord, teach me to pray.

Of Kindergarten and Crime

According to an Associated Press report, children at one Indianapolis kindergarten learned that the letter F is for Frisk!

As children arrived for kindergarten, security guards searched them with metal detectors to be sure they were not carrying weapons into class.

School officials explained that the kindergarten class met in a junior high school where students were searched for guns and knives. Officials were afraid older students would smuggle weapons into the building by concealing them on young children.

When students in junior high and even kindergarten have to be searched for weapons, it's time for major changes in our attitudes about violence and what is acceptable in our society. We adults must first eschew violence before we can expect our children to do the same.

Children learn from adults. Whether we want them to or not.

Peace I leave with you; My peace I give to you. (John 14–27)

Jesus, help adults avoid violence in speech, actions and amusements.

Happy Birthday
and Many Thanks

On his thirteenth birthday, a Japanese boy tradition-
ally receives a kite with his name on it. His friends and relatives joined in making a cord for the kite. They knot
string together, each person tying on a separate piece.

Before the boy flies this new kite, he looks at each
knot on the cord, thinking of the person who tied it.
Silently he gives thanks for all the things that person has
done for him. He takes time to remember the many ways
that others have helped him.

Any birthday would be a good time to remember
what others have done for us. Too often and too easily, we
take help for granted. Don't forget to say, "Thank you."

**Always and for everything [give] thanks in the
name of our Lord Jesus Christ to God the Father.
(Ephesians 5:20)**

*Indeed, Lord, thank You for all I am and have, all that You've
given me and especially thank You for Your Son.*

A Worship Tradition

Rosh Hashanah is the beginning of the new year on the Jewish calendar. At Temple B'nai Torah in Seattle, a century-old Torah just fourteen inches high is used at the children's services. Half the size of a regular Torah (a parchment scroll containing the Pentateuch, or first five books of the Hebrew Scriptures), it allows even small children to participate.

The little Torah made its way to America via New York's Ellis Island in 1909. Tuva Kastelman Gralnek had carried it from her hometown in what is now Belarus "so her children would have at least one source of Jewish instruction" in their new country.

Now her thoughtful piety is providing tradition and faith for new generations.

What are you doing to pass on your religious heritage to your children and future generations?

Keep these words that I am commanding you today in your heart. Recite them to your children and talk about them when you are at home and when you are away, when you lie down and when you rise. (Deuteronomy 6:6–7)

Thank You, Just Lawgiver, for Your Law of life and love.

"Thank God Each Day"

The late writer William Arthur Ward had some thought-provoking ideas on prayer you might consider:

"Wonderful things happen to us when we live expectantly, believe confidently, and pray affirmatively.

"Seeking to find how I should pray, this came to mind: Thank God each day.

"Prayer does not always bring us what we want; rather it helps us to become the kind of persons we should be.

"The value of prayer is not in what it gives us, but in what it makes us.

"It is not primarily a method of getting, but it is a splendid way of growing."

In one translation of Luke's Gospel Jesus is said to have spent a night "in communion with God." "Communion," is a definition of prayer from the heart, with the heart, to the heart of God.

Pray today.

[Jesus] went out to the mountain to pray. (Luke 6:12)

Jesus, teach me to go apart for prayer daily.

Admitting Mistakes

You may have heard of BBD&O, the legendary advertising agency. One of the founders, Bruce Barton, told this story about his working days as a young man.

He disagreed with his boss about something and offered facts to back up his opinion. His employer abruptly overruled him.

The next morning Barton got a call. "To my amazement it was the boss. Said he: 'I have been thinking about our discussion of yesterday, and I just want you to know you were right and I was wrong.'"

Barton continued, "Years have gone by and I have known all sorts and conditions of men and women. . . . They divide into two classes: those who feel they have lowered themselves by admitting a mistake, and so try in every way to rationalize it, and those who come out in forthright fashion and admit the facts."

Never be afraid to be honest with yourself. Never be afraid to apologize.

Take heart. (Matthew 9:2)

How liberating it is to be who I am: a person who can and does admit mistakes, Jesus.

Putting Books into Readers' Hands

Many good people do their best to encourage reading. Meet two.

Jacki Baker, owner of a bakery and ice cream store in Vermont, discovered that neighborhood children were not reading books. She set up an incentive program with prizes ranging from ice cream and cake to savings bonds. It worked. Parents soon reported that their "kids were holed up in their rooms reading."

Luis Orlando Murcia was a college student living in Jackson Heights, New York. He found that the local public library lacked material on his homeland, Colombia. He began a book drive. Within a year he had collected 1,700 volumes in English and Spanish on a variety of subjects, including his native land. The young man donated them to the library saying, "It is my way to say 'thank you, America.'"

Share a book. Spark an idea.

Nehemiah . . . founded a library and collected the books about the kings and prophets, and the writings of David. . . . In the same way Judas also collected all the books. (2 Maccabees 2:13–14)

Inspire readers to encourage others to enjoy reading, Holy Spirit.

Don't Count Your Chickens

Everybody loves a good story. Some are so entertaining and filled with wisdom that they withstand the test of time. *Aesop's Fables* are among them. Here's one of those ancient Greek tales that still bears repeating.

A milkmaid was given a pail of milk by the farmer as a reward. She knew a neighbor who would buy it and decided to buy some eggs with the money. These she planned to raise into chickens and then sell. Then she would buy herself some new clothes.

But the milkmaid's plans fall apart when she spills the milk. The moral of the story? Don't count your chickens before they're hatched.

Yet making plans and having dreams is not only normal, it's essential to a meaningful life. Don't let disappointments stop you. Work to make your dreams come true.

And remember, don't cry over spilt milk.

I will pour out My Spirit on all flesh. (Joel 2:28)

Encourage us to dream about a more just tomorrow, Spirit of God. And guide our efforts toward it.

Relief — for a Danger Missed

There's an old story about a respected and renowned teacher who was ordered by the king to go along on a bear hunt. He was terrified.

When he got back home, a neighbor asked him "How did the hunt go?"

"Wonderfully," said the teacher.

"How many bears did you see?" asked the neighbor.

"None," the teacher replied.

"None! Then how could the hunt have been wonderful?"

"When I'm hunting bears, seeing no bears is a wonderful experience."

It is all in your point of view.

Granted, it's hard to see any bright side to some situations. But, try to remember that keeping a positive point of view can make a huge difference in how you get through tough times.

Your all-powerful hand . . . did not lack the means to send upon them a multitude of bears. (Wisdom of Solomon 11:17)

On life's journey protect us, God our stronghold.

Porcine Paradise

Charles Town, West Virginia, is, for some of its residents, hog heaven.

Dale Riffle and Jim Brewer are the founders of PIGS – the Potbellied Pig Interest Group and Shelter – a sanctuary for 180 homeless and abused porkers.

The pigs are Vietnamese potbellied pigs, which were popular as pets in the 1980s. As time went by, many owners dumped the pigs because they grew larger than expected. As adults, they can ruin furniture and sometimes be aggressive with small children. Brewer and Riffle adopted the homeless pigs. They now live on five acres filled with plenty of mud puddles. The men hope to raise money so they can move to a bigger place and take in more unwanted pigs.

"I think we're all put on Earth for some reason," said Riffle. "I guess pigs are my lot in life."

We all have a special "lot in life," a mission, a job that is meant just for us. If we give it our best, we will have done all that God will ever ask of us.

Whenever we have an opportunity, let us work for the good of all. (Galatians 6:10)

Thank You, Holy Lord, for Earth and all its creatures.

Sagging Spirits

An early twentieth-century store window unintentionally showed a woman drunk at a dinner table.

One night, a window dresser finished a display showing mannequins arranged around a festive dinner table with the "hostess" raising her wine glass in a toast. But when he came in the next morning, the scene had changed.

At that time, the heads and chests of mannequins were made of wax. The electric lights used in the store window softened the wax. The "hostess" slumped over the table with her mouth sagging. Wine spilled from the glass in her limp hand. A surprising and unappealing scene.

There's nothing appealing about drinking when it gets out of control. If that happens, get help. You're worth it.

Be not among winebibbers . . . for the drunkard . . . will come to poverty. (Proverbs 23:20–21)

You've given us wine to cheer our hearts, Lord of the harvest. Help us never abuse it.

Nourished by Prayer

Rev. George Muller, a minister in nineteenth century England, had great faith in the miracles of prayer. Rev. Muller and his wife opened orphanages for destitute children, trusting that God would provide.

On one occasion, an orphanage had no food, but the children were, as usual, seated, waiting for breakfast. While Rev. Muller asked the blessing at the bare table, there was a knock at the door. It was the baker bringing bread. He said he had had a feeling the orphanage needed it. As soon as he left, a milkman knocked, offering cans of milk because his cart had broken down in front of the orphanage.

Prayers are not usually answered in such dramatic ways. But they are answered. You can be confident that God will guide and strengthen you when you ask for His help.

"I have compassion for the crowd, because they have been with Me now for three days and have nothing to eat. If I send them away hungry to their homes they will faint on the way – and some of them have come from a great distance." (Mark 8:2–3)

Jesus, remind me that You twice blessed bread and a few small fish to feed the hungry. May I never doubt Your compassion.

From Fear to Faith

During hard times, when we need to pray with great faith and trust, it would help to imitate the prophet Habakkuk. Here is the historical setting: It was the height of Babylonian power some six hundred years before Jesus. Habakkuk's nation had been overrun. Most of its people had been deported into slavery. Famine stalked the land.

Yet Habakkuk prayed:

> Though the fig tree does not blossom, and no fruit is on the vines; though the produce of the olive fails and the fields yield no food; though the flock is cut off from the fold and there is no herd in the stalls, yet I will rejoice in the Lord. I will exult in the God of my salvation. (Habakkuk 3:17–18)

If only we have a little of Habakkuk's trust! Pray for it. God will never desert you.

The earth will be filled with the knowledge of the glory of the Lord as the waters cover the sea. (Habakkuk 2:14)

Trust. Belief. Knowledge of Your glory. Whatever I call it, Lord, increase it — my trust, my belief, my knowledge of You.

A Matter of Perspective

People have told of seeing the shadow of a giant on Brocken Mountain in Germany.

The stories are true, but the giant is an illusion, a visual effect called the Brocken specter. Under certain conditions, a person standing on a mountain sees his own shadow, which the sun casts on clouds or fog.

The shadow appears larger than life-size, even as tall as the trees. Scientists think that since the shadow is flat, the eye can not judge size or distance accurately.

In everyday life, too, we can create our own monsters. For example, fear can make speaking in public seem terribly threatening. Think things through. Then prepare yourself. You can confront whatever monsters threaten you. And don't forget to put yourself in God's hands.

Why are you afraid? Have you no faith?
(Mark 4:40)

I want to trust, to have faith. God supply my lack.

Happy? Put Others First

Most of us want to be happy. We seek fulfillment, but all too often we do not seem to find it. In fact, there is a simple way. It comes by putting the focus on others.

Start by asking yourself, "What good can I do for someone today?" Consider all the people around you, at home, on the job, in your neighborhood. Then do something. It doesn't have to be a big favor, it can be as simple as a compliment on a job well done.

Then do something harder: be nice to a person you dislike or who dislikes you. It might be tough to do even a little thing, but a friendly gesture can help both of you.

Finally, single out a person you usually ignore and say or do something to make them feel special.

If you want to be happy yourself, be kind to others.

Hold unfailing your love for one another, since love covers a multitude of sins. (I Peter 4:8)

Spirit of the living God, how can I be kind today?

Unsettling Earthquakes

Earthquakes are terrifying not only because they are so dangerous but because they are also disorienting. They leave people without security, as the ground under their feet shakes or opens up. Sometimes it even dissolves.

During one Japanese earthquake several years ago, vibrations caused the particles of the wet, sandy soil under an apartment building to drift apart, turning into quicksand. The building tilted over onto its back, leaving residents floating in the liquefied soil.

Homeless people and refugees experience much the same trauma as earthquake victims. The world they knew has given way under their feet, leaving them without the security of home or country.

People who are trying to endure economic or political upheaval or natural disaster need help to endure as they as struggle to rebuild their lives. Do what you can to reach out.

Give, and it will be given to you. (Luke 6:38)

How may I lay a solid foundation for the afflicted, Lord of Mercy?

Indian Heritage and Pride

For years, Native Americans were made to feel so ashamed of their ethnic background that some even concealed it.

Happily, attitudes are changing. Today, an increasing number of people are identifying themselves as Native Americans.

Dan Thorn's grandmother destroyed her birth certificate to conceal the fact that she was a Native American. But Dan is tracing the family's roots and teaching his children about their Sioux heritage.

He says, "When the next census comes around, I'll put 'American Indian.' I'm very proud of that. I wish my grandmother could have been."

Each one of us is entitled to be proud of our own heritage. But never try to feel better about yourself at the expense of others.

Pursue righteousness, faith, love, and peace. . . . Have nothing to do with stupid and senseless controversies. (2 Timothy 2:22–23)

God, help me accept my own ethnic origins and others' with profound respect.

In Search of Beauty

Some plastic surgeons say teens now account for twenty-five percent of their business. Many teens are unhappy with their appearance and want to look like the season's top rock star or movie idol. Teens also think that changing their appearance will solve their low self-esteem.

In other cases surgery is done to reshape the nose, lips or eyelids to make them look like those of a different race. Believing that the features of one race are more attractive than those of another is absurd.

Lack of confidence and fear of being "different" come with adolescence. It's not surprising that teens should see cosmetic surgery as an instant panacea. But as maturity brings greater appreciation of individuality, they may regret that they rushed to change themselves.

Adults can help adolescents appreciate and accept the varieties of beauty, the wonderful individuality of God-given beauty. Start by being a good example of someone who appreciates your own uniqueness.

Wisdom and prudence . . . will be life for your soul and adornment for your neck. (Proverbs 3:22)

Help us to appreciate our own and others' unique beauty, Creator.

A Prayer of Praise and Gratitude

St. Teresa of Avila once wrote a litany of gratitude that reads in part:

> May you be blessed forever, Lord, for not abandon-
> ing me when I abandoned You.
> . . . for offering Your hand of love in my darkest,
> most lonely moment.
> . . . for putting up with such a stubborn soul.
> . . . for loving me more than I love myself.
> . . . for continuing to pour out Your blessing though
> I respond so poorly.
> . . . for drawing out the goodness in all people, even
> including me.
> . . . for repaying our sin with Your love.
> . . . for being constant and unchanging.
> . . . for Your countless blessings on me and on all
> Your creatures.

St. Teresa went beyond this litany of words to make her whole life a "litany of gratitude." Each of us has so very much for which to thank God, each moment of each hour.

"Stand up and bless the Lord your God."
(Nehemiah 9:5)

May all that is in me bless You, Merciful and Generous Lord.

A Garden of Knowledge

An old Arabian proverb describes a book as "a garden carried in a pocket." That's a pretty image. And it's true.

Some books offer the serenity and beauty of a garden. They offer a retreat from our everyday cares. Others offer a garden's variety, showing experiences outside of our own lives.

But the most important thing a book shares is ideas. Ideas may be as vibrant as a landscape of bright flowers, or as subtle as the perfume of a single blossom. But when coupled with our reflections they may lead us to wisdom.

That's a good reason to pick up a good book. Read it, think about it and share your thoughts and your books with others. Use your local library and encourage others to enjoy its possibilities.

[Make] your ear attentive to wisdom and [incline] your heart to understanding . . . cry out for insight, and raise your voice for understanding . . . then you will . . . find the knowledge of God. (Proverbs 2:1–5)

Enable me, Spirit of Wisdom, to seek You, to find You, and to embrace You.

Pick Yourself Up

During twelve years of international competition, figure-skater Paul Wylie had many falls, both literally and figuratively.

On his first jump in the 1988 Calgary Olympics, he fell and finished in tenth place. But in the years that followed, he kept competing. He barely got a spot on the 1992 Olympic team. Then in the Olympic warm-ups he fell again. But this time he went on to win a silver medal.

Wylie said, "I learned to overcome fear by relying on God's acceptance of me. . . . You know that God will use you whether you win or lose." When he failed, he told himself, "I'm going to learn from this."

Failure needn't be discouraging. Like Paul Wylie, we can learn from it.

Cast your burden on the Lord. (Psalm 55:22)

Redeemer, help me learn not to go it alone, but rather to lean on You.

Your Own Wonderful Life

During his illustrious acting career, James Stewart made many memorable films. The one he always called his personal favorite was Frank Capra's *It's a Wonderful Life.*

When the movie was released in 1947, it was not a box office success. Stewart believed it gained its great popularity in time because of the values it affirms: "love of hard work, love of community, love of country, and love of God."

The film tells the story of a good man facing personal disaster who gets to see what life would have been like for his loved ones if he had never been born. He learns that he has made a real difference in the lives of many people.

Perhaps that's the most basic reason for the film's continuing appeal. Each one of us needs an occasional reminder that we are important and that we can change the world for the better.

If you choose, you can keep the commandments, and to act faithfully is a matter of your own choice. (Sirach 15:15)

Enlighten and strengthen my will, God, so that by freely choosing to walk in Your way I can make this a better world.

Even Experts Can Fall

Gibbons are considered the most agile of all animals.

Although gibbons don't have tails, they have relatively long arms. And as they travel through the trees, they use their hands like hooks. They make long swings from branch to branch, covering as much as twenty-five or thirty feet in a single swing.

Yet even these champion tree-swingers fall often enough so that a quarter of the adult gibbon population has broken bones.

For gibbons and for people, falls or failures are a fact of life. The only way to avoid them would mean never doing anything at all. Don't be discouraged by failures. Remember, they're a part of learning. And so is healing.

Jesus spoke to them and said, "Take heart, it is I; do not be afraid." (Matthew 14:27)

Help me not to fear any failure except the failure to love You, Jesus.

Charting a Course for the Future

How far do you plan ahead?

In Matthew 6:34 we are admonished not to "worry about tomorrow, for tomorrow will bring worries of its own." We need to take time to smell the flowers.

However, a familiar slogan also reminds us that those who fail to plan, plan to fail. Perhaps emotionally we can live a day at a time, but otherwise we must prepare to build the life we want to live.

Where should we draw the line? How much of the future can we plan? How to strike a balance?

Only through prayer and in the knowledge of God's will can we get it right.

Trust God to direct you, your life, your plans, your hopes. Determine what you believe to be the Lord's will for you. Map the route to be taken, the steps necessary for achievement. Then let God shepherd you.

Take delight in the Lord, and He will give you the desires of your heart. Commit your way to the Lord; trust in Him, and He will act. (Psalm 37:4–5)

God, I do trust. Help my lack of trust!

Colorful Fall Foliage

Most years the fall foliage display in New England is spectacular. For a variety of climatic and geographic reasons, the leaves in New England take on greater brilliance than can be found elsewhere.

And this brings out the tourist in all of us. In New Hampshire, for instance, motel rooms for the weeks of the fall color change are often booked three years in advance by "Leaf Peepers." As the season progresses, calls to the tourist office mount until they number more than a thousand a day. People can't wait to enjoy the season's gorgeous show.

There is little to rival nature in her moods, whether those moods be angry, playful — or just serene. Are you aware of the beauty all around you? Nature's beauty can remind you of the perfect beauty of God.

From the greatness and beauty of created things comes a corresponding perception of their Creator. (Wisdom of Solomon 13:5)

Open my eyes to see Your beauty reflected in Creation, Maker-of-All.

Words Spoken
with Hearts and Hands

Father Patrick McCahill thinks it's just fine when his congregation doesn't utter a word of response during Mass.

Father McCahill offers a special Mass for the deaf at St. Elizabeth of Hungary Church in Manhattan. He speaks and signs at the same time, but the congregation responds only in sign language. Even choir members "sing" silently with their hands.

This special Mass enables the deaf to join fully in the worship service.

There are many other disabilities that make it hard to attend church. From use of a wheelchair to conditions such as Alzheimer's disease. But many congregations are finding ways to make churches and services more accessible, to open the doors of the church to all.

Is your place of worship doing all it can to welcome your neighbors with disabilities? Make a point of getting involved.

My brothers and sisters, do you with your acts of favoritism really believe in . . . Jesus Christ? . . . Have you not made distinctions among yourselves?
(James 2:1, 4)

Lord, whom we worship, enable us to make our houses of worship places of welcome and acceptance for each and all of Your children.

Nine Kinds of Trouble

Most of the things we fear never happen. President Calvin Coolidge once said, "If you see ten troubles coming down the road, you can be sure nine will run into a ditch before they reach you, and you'll have to battle with only one."

Fighting imaginary battles with the nine troubles we never meet can leave us physically and emotionally exhausted. We're so worn out from worry about problems that never materialize that it's hard for us to cope with the one problem we actually face.

Faith in God helps free us from the fears and worries that waste our time and energy and lets us use them productively, to solve real problems.

I, I am He who comforts you; why then are you afraid? (Isaiah 51:12)

Put Your arms around me, Lover of all, when trouble comes and I tremble with fear.

Ideals to Live By

These are some excerpts from the historic Charter of the United Nations that are worth consideration by individual men and women as well as by nations.

- We "reaffirm faith in fundamental human rights, in the dignity and worth of the human person, in the equal rights of men and women."
- We seek to "establish conditions under which justice and respect for the obligations arising from . . . law can be maintained."
- We seek "to promote social progress and better standards of life."
- We seek "to practice tolerance and [to] live together in peace with one another as good neighbors."

Can you imagine how much more humane our homes, offices, churches or synagogues; the stores and offices we frequent, would be were we to turn these excerpts into guidelines?

Hate evil and love good, and establish justice. (Amos 5:15)

Show me how to love You by loving my neighbor, dearest Lord.

Reach Out, Give Back

Make a Difference Day is a national promotion for volunteering.

Howard Waller was eager to volunteer. There was just one problem: He was serving five years in prison for fraud.

But Waller and seven other inmates obtained the approval of the warden to work with a church youth group. They finished renovations on a home for abused boys. Waller was also asked to volunteer at the home, to relate his mistakes and experiences to young people.

His wife says this opportunity to help others has given him a new outlook on life.

Waller commented, "People think prisoners only take from society. I saw Make a Difference Day as a chance to give back."

Volunteer work is a good way to experience the satisfaction of helping others as you help yourself.

Do not neglect to do good and to share what you have, for such sacrifices are pleasing to God. (Hebrews 3:16)

Lord, enable me to find satisfaction in helping others in Your Name.

Reconciling Ourselves

Consider this story about reconciliation. It seems that a fight began when a man, riding a bicycle with a basket of oranges balanced on the handlebars, collided with a heavily burdened porter.

The oranges scattered. Insults flew. The porter clenched his fists and moved toward the bicyclist. A crowd gathered.

Then a ragged man stepped from the crowd and kissed the porter's clenched fists. Approving murmurs rose from the crowd. The bicyclist and the porter started to relax. People began to collect the scattered oranges.

How willing are any of us to be humble, to seek reconciliation? It's something worth pursuing – peace and good will among neighbors and strangers, friends and family.

Be reconciled to your brother or sister. (Matthew 5:24)

Encourage us to be reconciled to each other for the sake of peace, forgiving God.

On Complaints and Listening

Large corporations are finding that it pays to listen to people.

Many companies now include a toll-free consumer hot-line number with their products. The tens of thousands of people who call each day have the satisfaction of getting information immediately, or of knowing that their complaints are really heard.

And the companies not only learn about defects that need correcting, they get information that's helpful in marketing products.

If dialogue is proving valuable in business, it's even more important in everyday life. When people really listen to one another, everybody benefits.

Sacrifice . . . you do not desire, but you have given me an open ear. (Psalm 40:6)

Open my ears to really hear You, Lord, my own self and others.

Lost in Time

On a day when you haven't accomplished much, have you ever felt that you've just lost a day? On occasion, people have really lost days.

The Julian calendar, introduced in 46 B.C., was not exact, and lost a day every 128 years. Gradually, it got out of phase with the seasons.

So when the Gregorian calendar that we now use was adopted by much of Europe in 1582, there was a difference of ten days. The days were just dropped. That year, the day following October 4 became October 15. Later, when the English finally adopted the Gregorian calendar, they lost eleven days.

Many of us "lose" time in a different sense by procrastinating. Try to find time for things that truly matter to you and those you love.

You, beloved, are not in darkness, for that day to surprise you like a thief . . . let us not fall asleep as others do, but let us keep awake and be sober. (I Thessalonians 5:4–6)

Indeed You have made me a child of the light, Jesus. Help me stay alert.

On Holy Ground

Fred Rogers is not only the creator of *Mr. Rogers' Neighborhood*, the long-running children's television series, he is also an ordained minister.

As a seminary student, he made a habit of attending different churches in order to hear many preaching styles. One Sunday he endured "the most poorly crafted sermon I had ever heard in my life." But then Fred Rogers realized that the friend who had attended with him had tears in her eyes. Her experience was just the opposite of his. She had found just what she needed that day.

Fred Rogers says, "That's when I realized that the space between someone doing the best he or she can and someone in need is holy ground. . . . The Holy Spirit had transformed that feeble sermon for her — and as it turned out — for me, too."

Sometimes, just seeing or hearing things from another perspective can transform our judgments.

All things come in pairs, one opposite the other. . . . Each supplements the virtues of the other. (Sirach 42:24–25)

As You respect my free will and intelligence, God, so may I respect others'.

A Toast to Opportunity

Champagne, with its sparkling effervescence, is associated with joyous celebrations.

Three centuries ago, Dom Perignon, a blind Benedictine monk, began making this wine by accident.

Dom Perignon was in charge of the wine cellars at an abbey in the Champagne region of France. One day he tried sealing wine bottles with cork instead of the oil-soaked cloth used to seal bottles then. The cloth let the carbon dioxide produced during fermentation escape, but the cork kept it in. The result was a sparkling wine.

To keep the sparkle of joy in your life, capture each day's opportunities. Do not squander your time and energy on regrets or worries. Trust God to forgive your mistakes of yesterday and help you with the problems of tomorrow.

Just do your best to let today sparkle.

He does not deal with us according to our sins, nor repay us according to our iniquities. (Psalm 103:10)

Forgiving Lord, show us how to learn from our sins and mistakes and move on into joy.

What Goes Up . . .

A hill in Lake Wales, Florida, is known as Spook Hill because cars, bikes, and skateboards coast up the hill instead of down. Water, too, flows uphill.

Citrus farmers in the small community long ago gave up planting trees near the hill because visitors kept pulling off the oranges so they could watch them roll uphill.

There are several legends about the hill. Some say it is haunted by the ghost of a Seminole chief trying to save people from the swamps where evil spirits and alligators lurk. Others say that the ghosts of pirates are attempting to call attention to buried treasure.

Geologists speculate that asteroids may have deposited magnetic material there millions of years ago (although no metal deposits worth mining have been found); another, it's a gravitational anomaly caused by varying densities in bedrock.

But no one really knows the cause of the strange phenomenon at Spook Hill.

How limited our knowledge is . . . how much of God's Creation remains beyond our comprehension!

How desirable are all His works, and how sparkling they are to see! . . . Who could ever tire of seeing His glory? (Sirach 42:22, 25)

That I might rejoice in Your Creation as a gentle reminder that I, too, am Your creation guarded as the apple of Your eye.

Find Your Place
Among the Saints

What — or better, who — are saints?

Nuns, priests, deacons, bishops, popes, cardinals, missionaries, contemplatives, liturgists?

Sometimes. But religious life is not a prerequisite for holiness.

Catherine Fieschi Adorno ran a hospital. Thomas More was a politician, a lawyer and the Lord Chancellor of England. Margaret of Scotland was a queen, wife and the mother of ten children. Isadore and Maria were Spanish farmers. Native American Kateri Tekawitha, who became known as the Lily of the Mohawks, was a young woman who practiced being a good neighbor and living a whole-souled life.

Saints, in other words, are people who live up to the grace of their baptism. Some are famous within their own lifetimes. But more spend ordinary lives quietly, yet extra-ordinarily, and die in their own beds surrounded by family and friends.

Saints are people who realize that they are children of God and treat others the same way.

**In Your presence there is fullness of joy.
(Psalm 16:11)**

Jesus, help me to live Your law of love in the unspectacular ordinariness of my daily life.

Warm Heart, Warm Hands

The late Michael Greenberg was known among New York City's homeless as "Gloves." Every winter for thirty years, he gave warm gloves to the poor.

As a boy Greenberg helped his father take baked goods to market every morning before dawn. He wheeled them in a pushcart. Life wasn't easy for the family, but Greenberg's father told him, "Don't deprive yourself of the joy of giving." When his father died, he decided to honor his memory.

Instead of just donating gloves to missions and soup kitchens, Greenberg handed them out on the street. He wanted to talk with the homeless. He said, "It's not so much the gloves, but telling people they count."

Michael Greenberg gave more than gloves. He gave of himself. What better legacy could any of us leave?

Since there will never cease to be some in need on the earth, I therefore command you, "Open your hand to the poor and needy." (Deuteronomy 15:11)

God, help me imitate Your generosity to me.

The Right Question

Some questions, however well-intentioned, are better left unasked. That's the opinion of psychologist, writer, and lecturer, Eda LeShan.

She's also a woman who has lived a long life, who has suffered a heart attack, two strokes and four operations. Dr. LeShan says that she is tired of being asked, "How do you feel?" She prefers: "What are you doing?"

"When we can tell someone what we're doing instead of how, it affirms our sense of being complete persons who aren't identified by our infirmities," says Dr. LeShan.

"Feeling well and being intensely active is the good fortune of many older people. But those of us who've not been so blessed crave the pleasure and reassurance that comes with being valued for what we are still able to do."

Do as much, be as much, as you can. Whatever your age, live each day as fully and beautifully as possible.

Teach us to count our days that we may gain a wise heart. (Psalm 90:12)

Help me, generous Lord, to treasure the days of my life and to use them to do good for Your people.

Where the Potato Is King

When you think of potatoes you are likely to think of Maine or Idaho or Ireland. But you might as well think of China or India or Peru, the homeland of the potato. Potatoes are cultivated in another 126 countries, too.

Peru is the site of the International Potato Center where research on the tuber is conducted. Many unusual varieties of potatoes, ones with blue-purple flesh and skin, and red-fleshed ones with rosy skin, for example, are still grown in the Andes Mountains where potatoes originated.

There is increasing interest in the potato because agricultural experts believe it has the potential for helping the world feed itself. Potatoes, it seems, can now be grown from seeds instead of "eyes" (slices of seed potatoes containing buds). Too, the potato is rich in fiber, protein, potassium, iron, magnesium and vitamin C.

We are still in an age of discovery. But discovery is not for scientists only. Every day presents us with fresh opportunities to discover new things about our own environment, about other people and about ourselves. Often, that means digging to find the buried treasure. It's worth it. Be a discoverer.

O Lord, how manifold are your works! In wisdom You have made them all. (Psalm 104:24)

Open my eyes to wonders of Your creation, the wonders of my very being, Creator.

The Difference Between Price and Value

Tulips had become the rage in seventeenth century Holland and were in such demand that bulbs of some varieties were literally worth their weight in gold. In 1636, three rare tulip bulbs sold for enough to buy a house. In hopes of getting rich quick, people sold their belongings and invested in bulbs. But the tulip craze lasted only a few years. Then the market crashed, bringing financial ruin to speculators.

Fads still determine the value of many objects.

Young people, with their fear of being different, are likely to attach great importance to whatever is currently in style. Jerrold Anderson, writing in *The Chicago Tribune*, said, "You know something is wrong when students today are more concerned about the name on their shoes than the name on their schoolbooks."

Your example sends young people a message about values. Be sure it's the message you want them to receive.

Wealth hastily gotten will dwindle, but those who gather little by little will increase it. (Proverbs 13:12)

Help me teach eternal values by the way I live and the choices I make each day, Holy Wisdom.

Another Way to Win a Race

Doctors told the late Fred Lebow that he had only a few months to live after he was diagnosed with brain cancer. Lebow, who was the director of the New York City Marathon, decided to prove them wrong.

He decided to run in the 1992 marathon. The race ran through 26 miles of New York City and included close to 26,000 runners. Lebow had not run in the Marathon since the early 1970's when it was a race held inside Central Park with fewer than 100 runners.

Spectators cheered and cried as Fred Lebow crossed the finish fine with a time of 5 hours, 32 minutes and 34 seconds. He had fulfilled his dream.

You can overcome obstacles when you believe that you can. It is when you give up on yourself that you miss out on the truly great challenges and achievements in life.

Because you have made the Lord your refuge, the Most High your dwelling place, no evil shall befall you, no scourge come near your tent. (Psalm 91:9)

God my protector, help me know that You guard and strengthen me.

The Value of a Vote

If you have ever thought that it's just too much trouble to vote on election day, don't say that to Marian Young.

Entering the voting booth one election day, she made the mistake of moving the lever for the curtain back and forth. She had in effect voted without casting her ballot.

The only way for her to get a second chance was to get a court order. Armed with a certificate from polling officials she went to the State Supreme Court.

After being sent to several offices, Miss Young was finally granted a hearing. And when the court order was granted, the judge told her that voting "is worth the effort you have taken today. . . . If I were wearing a hat I would take it off to you."

Marian Young cast her vote in triumph.

How much is your right, your privilege to vote worth to you?

We cannot keep from speaking about what we have seen and heard. (Acts 4:20)

Holy Spirit, give me the wisdom to vote for those who will serve Your people.

Mary's Little Lamb Revisited

Remember the nursery rhyme, "Mary had a little lamb/its fleece was white as snow / and everywhere that Mary went / the lamb was sure to go"? Well, there was a real Mary, Mary Sawyer of Sterling, Massachusetts. According to the local historical society, Mary's lamb followed her to school one day in 1816. Mary hid the lamb under her desk. All went well until Mary was called to the front of the class for a recitation. The lamb followed and was banished to a nearby shed until dismissal.

John Roulstone, who was visiting the school that day remembered Mary and her pet lamb in verse. Fourteen years later, editor Sara Josepha Hale, included Roulstone's work in a book of poetry and added several more verses of her own.

Today Mary and her lamb live on – in the verse and in a statue of the two on Boston Commons.

Childhood offers many memories. Write down a memory that is dear to you. Make it a habit. It will bring pleasure to you and provide a keepsake for your family.

The poor man had . . . one little ewe lamb . . . it grew up with him and with his children; it used to eat of his meager fare, and drink from his cup, and lie in his bosom, and it was like a daughter to him. (2 Samuel 12:3)

May my memories be a source of growth, insight and even healing, God.

An Appreciation of Happiness

Here's one definition of happiness:

Happiness is . . . going to sleep at peace with your
self and the world.
Having a new book, whether borrowed from the
library or bought.
Picking up autumn leaves to admire their beauty.
Being at home with the lights on just at twilight.
Bundling up against the winter's cold to take a
refreshing walk.
The slow, silent fall of soft, white snow.
Reflecting on the past, enjoying the present, antici-
pating the future.

How would *you* define happiness? It has been said
that, "we carry the seed of happiness within our own
minds." Nurture that seed today and each and every day.

Happy are those who find wisdom.
(Proverbs 3:13)

Teach us wisdom, root of happiness, Holy Spirit.

Creativity Is Ageless

At the time Beatrice Wood received the American Craft Council's gold medal for highest achievement in craftsmanship, her ceramics were in the permanent collections of a dozen major American museums from coast-to-coast.

Interestingly, her career began when she was forty and couldn't find a teapot to match some plates she had bought.

A friend suggested that she take a ceramics class at a local high school so that she could make a matching teapot. And with that simple start, her talent and hard work fashioned a respected reputation for beautiful designs.

Age may tell us where we are in life chronologically. But age can never tell us who we are. Who we are comes from within. Today, create as beautiful a day as you can for yourself and those around you.

Riches are inappropriate for a small-minded person; and of what use is wealth to a miser? . . . If one is mean to himself, to whom will he be generous? . . . No one is worse than one who is grudging to himself. (Sirach 14:3, 5, 14)

Today enable me to treat myself to the beautiful day You've prepared for me, Creator.

The Measure of Greatness

There's nothing new about people wanting and working to achieve greatness. Power, fame, prestige, are the words that one associates with the concept of greatness.

But Ben Franklin had another idea in mind. In 1729 he wrote, "If we were as industrious to become good as to make ourselves great, we should become really great by being good, and the number of valuable people would be much increased.

"But it is a grand mistake to think of being great without goodness," he continued. "And I pronounce it as certain, that there was never yet a truly great person who was not at the same time truly virtuous."

Ben Franklin's definition offers a lot to think about. Which is more important: knowing you are trying to be as good as possible? Or being judged great by others who do not know whether or not you really are good?

If riches are a desirable possession in life, what is richer than wisdom? (Wisdom of Solomon 8:5)

Enable us to judge our actions and values by Your standards, Holy Spirit.

A Lesson in Giving

A homeless man taught teenager Nassar Stoertz a lesson in giving.

Nassar was selling fruit baskets. A homeless man asked why he was selling them. Nassar explained that he was raising money to build a playground for handicapped children. The man said he wanted to help. He couldn't buy a basket, but he gave Nassar all he had — one dollar.

The teenager didn't want to take it, knowing that the man must need it for food. But the man insisted, saying, "What you give will come back to you." Later that night he came by to tell the teen that a policeman had given him a meal.

What we give does come back to us. Not necessarily in material goods, but in the satisfaction that comes from helping others.

In everything do to others as you would have them do to you; for this is the law and the prophets. (Matthew 7:12)

Do I treat others as I want to be treated, Lord?

Books Beyond Price

David Brown, a lawyer fascinated by archeology, was doing field research in Old Harbor, Alaska. One night he went looking for the library. But he learned that it had been destroyed by fire. There was a room available for a library, but no money for books.

On his return, he spoke to Pound Ridge, New York, teacher Nancy Freiheit and she to Marilyn Tinter, the library director. They decided to help out. Sales of surplus and donated books are now held every two months. Proceeds go to the Old Harbor, Alaska, library.

Emily Capjohn, the Old Harbor librarian, says, "We appreciate it so much. They're just wonderful."

Indeed, sharing is wonderful. And all it takes to get the ball rolling is one person willing to see a problem and get others involved in finding a solution.

Those who despise their neighbors are sinners, but happy are those who are kind to the poor. (Proverbs 14:21)

Generous Lord, help us grow through sharing our time, talents and treasure.

Surprise Gift of Love

One November, Alice and Bob Blair, the parents of eleven children, were expecting another child. Sadly, the baby died and Alice Blair developed pneumonia.

Three days before Alice was sent home from the hospital a neighbor who owned a craft shop called Bob Blair. Would he bring all the children to spend a day with her?

"Mom," the children cried the day their mother finally came home, "do we have a surprise for you!" There, on the mantle above the fireplace was a Nativity scene cast from clay.

Each child told what part he or she had played in its creation. Even two-year-old Ginger said, "I made the Baby Jesus." Thirty years later, Alice Blair says that that Nativity scene "remains one of my most precious gifts."

Indeed, love makes a gift memorable, not its cost.

I have loved you with an everlasting love; therefore I have continued my faithfulness to you. (Jeremiah 31:3)

Yes, Father, You loved me so much You gave Your Son as my Savior. Thank You.

Appreciating Another's Talent

John Tyndall was a world acclaimed nineteenth-century English physicist.

Tyndall also respected the accomplishments of others. He once testified in a patent lawsuit. The physicist told how he and Thomas Edison had followed the same process of experimentation, but he had stopped short of the final, successful step which Edison had taken.

A lawyer who did not appreciate the difficulties of scientific research asked, "When the next step was so obvious, why did you not take it?"

Tyndall replied, "Because I was not Thomas Edison."

Value your own God-given abilities and talents. And never fail to generously recognize the gifts of others.

What are human beings that You are mindful of them, mortals that You care for them? Yet You have made them a little lower than God, and . . . given them dominion over the works of Your hands. (Psalm 8:4–6)

Thank You, Creator, for giving me so much — especially the gift of being made in Your image and likeness.

Conflict for the Better

Conflicting opinions, whether between individuals or groups, isn't always bad. In fact, things would be pretty dull if people always agreed about everything.

You can make conflict constructive if you draw on abilities and talents you might not even realize you have in finding new ways to deal with problems.

Let conflict stimulate your interest in community and world affairs. Use it to clarify your views on particular subjects and why others have opposing views.

In short, conflict can result in personal growth and increase your understanding of other people's ideas and feelings — if you let it.

The next time a dispute arises, use it as an opportunity to learn and grow. Try to settle it amicably, respecting the rights and opinions of all.

Jesus entered the temple and drove out all who were selling and buying . . . and He overturned the tables of the money changers and the seats of those who sold doves. (Matthew 21:12)

Teach me not to shy from conflict when it's necessary, Jesus.

Hope in the Morning

Oscar Hammerstein is one of the legendary figures of the American musical theater. Along with Richard Rogers he wrote classic shows such as *Oklahoma, South Pacific, The King and I,* and *The Sound of Music.*

Each has some serious undertones, but the writer was still occasionally criticized for the pure entertainment of his musical comedies. Hammerstein felt no need to apologize. "I know the world is filled with troubles and many injustices," he said. "But reality is as beautiful as it is ugly. I think it is just as important to sing about beautiful mornings as it is to talk about slums. I just couldn't write anything without hope in it."

Life without hope is deadly to the spirit. With hope all things are possible.

Hope deferred makes the heart sick.
(Proverbs 13:12)

Redeemer, we do hope in Your loving kindness. Increase our hope.

A Different Vision

When you consider the wide range of colors you can see, it's awe-inspiring to realize that there are still other colors you can not see.

Scientists tell us that insects, for instance, see a different range of colors from human beings. To a bee, a red flower just looks black. But the bee can see ultraviolet, a color invisible to our eyes. So a flower that looks drab to us may glow with color to a bee.

Insects can also detect polarization. This means that sunlight coming from different directions at different hours of the day has distinct qualities.

Next time you're feeling bored, take a minute to think about the amazing world around you. Experience the joy of God's wondrous Creation. And offer a word of appreciation to your Maker.

God saw everything that He made, and indeed, it was very good. (Genesis 1:31)

Thank You for the light to see Your beautiful, vivid and vibrant world, Creator.

Jefferson's Rules for Living

On her twelfth birthday, Cornelia Jefferson Randolph received a letter from her grandfather that she often reread. Thomas Jefferson told his granddaughter that the "Canons of Conduct in Life" were:

1. Never put off to tomorrow what you can do today.
2. Never trouble another with what you can do yourself.
3. Never spend your money before you have it.
4. Never buy a thing you do not want because it is cheap.
5. Take care of your cents. Dollars will take care of themselves.
6. Pride costs more than hunger, thirst and cold.
7. We never repent of eating too little.
8. Nothing is troublesome that one does willingly.
9. When angry, count to ten before you speak, if very angry, count to one hundred.

These "canons" show Jefferson's high regard for the ideals of perseverance, moderation, patience and respect. Cultivating and living them is at least as difficult now as in Thomas Jefferson's day, but they are still worthy goals.

Teach me Your way, O Lord. (Psalm 86:11)

Show me Your way, Lord.

Prospecting for Peace

During the California gold rush, Daniel Pound may have been the only prospector who didn't want to find gold.

All he really wanted was solitude. He pretended to look for gold as an excuse to stay alone in the mountains without being considered strange.

Once a serious prospector happened to come to Pound's camp. He cried, "You've got gold here!" At this unwelcome news, Pound loaded up his belongings and moved farther into the mountains. What he valued was not gold but peace and quiet.

There are times when all of us would like to retreat to the mountains. Unfortunately, that's rarely possible. But a few minutes of quiet meditation can help restore inner peace.

[Jesus] would withdraw to deserted places and pray. (Luke 5:16)

Jesus, enable me to make time for solitary prayer.

Concrete Idea Paves the Way

The town of Bellefontaine, Ohio, literally paved the way for a revolution in transportation.

Thanks to the ideas of George Bartholomew, this town had the first concrete streets in America — before gasoline-fueled "horseless carriages" were even in use.

Bartholomew came up with a special formula for cement. He persuaded skeptical town officials to let him pave the main streets by donating materials and labor for the first section.

These improved streets, built in the 1890s, opened new possibilities and helped spark the development of the automobile industry.

Important changes often begin with the creativity of one person. Keep your mind open to new ideas. Cultivate your own creativity.

Happy is the person who meditates on wisdom and reasons intelligently, who reflects . . . on her ways and ponders her secrets, pursuing her like a hunter and lying in wait on her paths. (Sirach 14:20–22)

Holy Spirit, font of wisdom, give me a share of Your wisdom.

Warm Hospitality

Hospitality is not necessarily related to lavish enter-taining. Nineteenth century writer Henry David Thoreau put it this way:

"I sat at a table where were rich food and wine in abundance, and obsequious attendance, but sincerity and truth were not; and I went away hungry from the inhos-pitable board. The hospitality was as cold as the ices. I thought there was no need of ice to freeze them. They talked to me of the age of the wine and fame of the vin-tage; but I thought of . . . purer wine, of a more glorious vintage, which they had not got, and could not buy."

Share the wine of "glorious vintage" with family, friends, even strangers. Hospitality that's rich in warmth and sincerity and goodwill goes as well with frankfurters as with filet mignon.

Better is a dinner of vegetables where love is than a fatted ox and hatred with it. (Proverbs 15:17)

May my hospitality be warm and welcoming, Jesus.

Talking Turkey

What do we know about the first Thanksgiving?

Well, we know that this feast was held in 1621 to mark the Pilgrims' first harvest. We know, too, that the meal was eaten outdoors, that Native Americans and Pilgrims dined together, and that turkey and pumpkin found their way to the table.

The most important fact we know about the fall feast has little to do with guests or food; it is a fact about feeling. Wrote Edward Winslow, a partaker of that meal: ". . . by the goodness of God, we are so far from want that we often wish you partakers of our plenty."

Although the Pilgrims did not celebrate this feast each year, we can be fairly certain that often throughout the years that followed they took stock of their lives, thanking God for His goodness in offering them plenty — and praying that His bounty be given to those especially in need.

O give thanks to the Lord of lords, for He is good, for His steadfast love endures forever . . . [who] rescued us from our foes . . . who gives food to all flesh, for His steadfast love endures forever. (Psalm 136:3, 24–25)

Unite all citizens of every race and creed in one hymn of thanksgiving to You, sustaining Lord.

Thanks, Good Neighbor

Terri Melrose and her husband were involved in a minor Thanksgiving weekend auto accident. Police officer Wayne Meers brought them to his own home.

His wife Nancy welcomed them and helped them make necessary phone calls. She drove the Melroses to the local hospital and then to a pharmacy and their hotel.

Mrs. Meers told the Melroses to call at any hour, no matter how late, if they awakened hungry.

Terri Melrose says, "She gave us much-needed hugs before she left."

There are many ways to be a Good Samaritan. Choose your own way, but just be sure to choose to love your neighbor.

The compassion of human beings is for their neighbors, but the compassion of the Lord is for every living thing. (Sirach 18:13)

Divine Physician, who needs my compassion, tenderness and understanding?

Personal Disaster Plan

Judith Martin, who writes the etiquette column "Miss Manners," had an eye-catching opening line one day. It read: "In case of disaster, reach first for etiquette."

She went on to say that even among people who deny the value of etiquette in their everyday lives, a high standard is often practiced in times of emergency.

While one of the standard excuses for rudeness is stress, in truly life-threatening situations, many, in fact, most, people act with courtesy and courage.

During the World Trade Center bombing evacuation, "People not only proceeded in an orderly fashion down the smoke-filled stairs, but they yielded to those more obviously in need of assistance, such as pregnant women."

That's something to ponder the next time we are less than kind — with no excuse at all.

He who pursues righteousness and kindness will find life and honor. (Proverbs 21:21)

Holy Spirit, show me how to be kind when I feel like it and when I don't.

Defining Success

Robert Louis Stevenson was a man of great literary ability as well as one of faith and deep human insight. Here is an adaptation of his definition of success:

> That person is a success who has lived well, laughed often and loved much;
> who has gained the respect of intelligent people, and the love of children;
> who has filled a unique niche and accomplished his or her task;
> who leaves the world better than before, whether by a perfect poem or a rescued soul; who never lacked appreciation of the earth's beauty or failed to express it; who looked for the best in others
> and gave the best he or she had.

Success means different things to different people. Write a few lines about your own idea of success. It will tell you about yourself and your standards, and where change might be needed if you wish to be a success in the eyes of yourself, your God, your friends, your family.

What does it profit them if they gain the whole world, but lose or forfeit themselves? (Luke 9:25)

Jesus, give me the grace to live Your definition of success.

Setting and Meeting Goals

Sasha Young, a junior at Great Bridge High School in Chesapeake, Virginia, just may have set a precedent. The young woman rode in the homecoming parade as part of the queen's court, and then went off to play for her high school football team.

Sasha is the starting kicker for the team and the first female football player for the Great Bridge Wildcats. She tried out for the team just like everyone else and is capable of kicking thirty-yard field goals.

She proved herself to the rest of the team through her accuracy and consistency. In turn, they all voted for her to be on the homecoming court.

There may be times in your life when people will tell you that you are not capable of doing something because of your age, your gender, or a physical handicap. Take a risk and prove yourself.

O Lord, we beseech You, give us success. (Psalm 118:25)

You want me to be successful here and hereafter, Lord. In fact, You hold out the means of success to me.

Familiar Feelings

The problems a mother polar bear in the New York Zoological Garden, better known as the Bronx Zoo, was having with her cub one day were painfully familiar to the human parents watching.

The mother bear was trying to coax the cub into the water for swimming practice. But it refused. When the mother bear persisted, nudging her offspring toward the water, it began hitting and kicking her. For a long time, the mother patiently ignored the cub's behavior. But finally, when the young bear kicked her in the face, she gently but firmly cuffed it.

Children, too, can be adorable one minute and wildly frustrating the next. Human parents know that a child's misbehavior is no excuse for hitting a child. And, they are well aware of the patience needed to teach, guide, and discipline children in a firm, loving, yet always non-abusive way.

Being a parent is not always easy, but it is always consequential.

Listen, children . . . and be attentive, that you may gain insight. (Proverbs 4:1)

Enable us, Father – Creator, to see children as the gifts from You that they are.

Failing, Trying, Trying Again

What seem like failures are often steps to success.

On his way home from the 1851 London Exhibition, American inventor Gail Borden noticed that children on board had no milk because the cows were seasick. He began to think about how to create a stable, readily accessible milk supply.

Later, on a visit to a Shaker community, he saw vacuum pans being used to condense fruit juices. He tried using one to condense milk. He worked for three years before he perfected the process.

When he started a condensed milk company, it failed. He tried again. Finally, during the Civil War, condensed milk became popular as an army ration. After the war, sales boomed.

Borden's epitaph reads: "I tried and failed; I tried again and again and succeeded."

May God grant us the grace to learn from failure.

Human success is in the hand of the Lord. (Sirach 10:5)

Thank You, Redeemer, for my successes in the past. Give me the wisdom to rely on You for future successes.

Someone with Whom to Talk

Every job has its stresses. But the work demands on police officers can cause particular problems. Where does a cop go to talk over troubles?

In Orlando, Florida, a group of volunteer chaplains provide the answer. They listen to officers, radio dispatchers, 911 operators, all the people in the police department who deal with crises and tragedies on a daily basis. These chaplains take basic training and ride in squad cars to get closer to the officers.

Chaplain Jack Day believes that "confidentiality is important. It's good to be right with the officer because you get a chance to walk in his shoes. When you walk in someone's shoes, you find out how it feels to be in his or her position."

Most of us like to think we are understanding of human nature with all its foibles. But putting ourselves in the other person's place, recognizing feelings, needs and problems are the first steps to empathy and compassion.

You shall not render an unjust judgment; you shall not be partial to the poor or defer to the great: with justice you shall you judge your neighbor. (Leviticus 19:15)

Open my eyes to see the world through my neighbor's eyes, Holy Spirit.

The 1,200-Pound Donation

Katie Alward of Granby, Connecticut, is a 4-H Club member. She bought an Angus crossbreed called Black Velvet. And she trained, fed and cared for the steer every day for eighteen months. "He was an extra sweet animal," she says.

She entered the then 1,200 pound Black Velvet in the West Springfield, Massachusetts, fair. He was named "Reserve Champion" – second among sixty steers.

Afterwards, Katie Alward donated the steer to St. Elizabeth House, a shelter and soup kitchen in Hartford, Connecticut. Paul Laffin, associate director, said, "This really redefines the phrase 'Holy Cow.'"

Black Velvet's 1,200 pounds yielded 550 pounds of quality meat for the poor and homeless.

All of us can use our creativity to offer something to charity, to people. Our talents, time and treasure are gifts to be shared with others.

A little with righteousness is better than wealth with wrongdoing . . . Almsgiving saves from death and purges away every sin. (Tobit 12:8–9)

What can I donate to charity from all You've given me, Lord God?

True Joy in Giving

Most adults enjoy giving presents to children and seeing their pleasure in receiving them. But children also need an opportunity to learn the joy of giving.

One day a woman and little girl of about three stood listening to a blind violinist in a New York subway station. When the violinist finished playing a number, the woman handed the little girl a coin and she ran over to the musician. The child's face was glowing with pleasure as she presented her gift.

In Thailand, youngsters are routinely taught charitable giving. On a child's birthday, he or she gives presents instead of receiving them. A child, for instance, may give food to a monk.

We do children a great service when we help them learn the joy of giving, just as we also help them learn how to receive with gratitude.

Whoever receives one such child in My name welcomes Me, and whoever welcomes Me, welcomes . . . the One who sent Me. (Mark 9:37)

Show us how to extend a heartfelt welcome to children, Child Jesus.

Clay in the Hand of the Potter

When you think of saints, the name of Irenaeus may not be the first to leap to mind. In fact, this second century bishop of what is now France is considered the first great Christian theologian. Irenaeus still offers ideas worth contemplating, like these:

"It is not you who shape God; it is God who shapes you.

"If then you are the handiwork of God, await the hand of the Artist who does all things in due season.

"Offer the pottery of your heart, soft and tractable, and keep well the form in which the Artist has fashioned you.

"Let your clay be moist, lest you grow hard and lose the imprint of the Potter's fingers."

That's a marvelous and comforting image: a lump of clay in the process of creation marked by the hand of the Maker, warm from His touch, malleable to His design.

Like clay in the hand of the potter, to be molded as he pleases, so all are in the hand of their Maker. (Sirach 33:13)

Hold me always in the hollow of Your hand, Divine Potter.

Pause a Moment for Thanks

It's easy to take for granted the less than spectacular ways that our lives have been touched and blessed by all God's creation, all His creatures.

Poet Rabindranath Tagore expressed it this way: "I have thanked the trees that have made my life fruitful but have failed to remember the grass that has ever kept it green."

We gratefully acknowledge the help of the doctor who performs a difficult operation or the friend who lends us money for a mortgage payment.

But we might overlook the salesclerk who goes to great trouble to find what we need or the neighbor who picks up the children when we are running late.

Let's not forget to express our thanks for the small but important things other people do to help us. And to return the favor by aiding others in their daily lives.

As you therefore have received Christ Jesus the Lord, continue to live your lives in Him, rooted and built up in Him and established in the faith . . . abounding in thanksgiving. (Colossians 2:6–7)

Put a song of thanksgiving on my lips, Christ Jesus.

Sharing Our Blessings

One of the big, bright, beautiful annual Christmas trees to grace the holiday season at Manhattan's Rockefeller Center brought with it a special blessing. For more than sixty years, the majestic Norway spruce graced the lawn of the convent of the Sisters of Christian Charity in Mendham, New Jersey.

Those in charge of selecting trees for Rockefeller Center had long wanted the seventy-five-foot tree. After one particularly stormy winter, the nuns, afraid that another such winter might topple the tree, decided to let it be taken down. But before their tree was cut, the nuns blessed it.

"We have mixed emotions," said one of the sisters. "We'll miss the tree, but we're happy it will give so many people pleasure."

In joyous celebration we remember Christ's birth. And in sharing our blessings with others, we remember His love.

Though He was rich, yet for your sakes [our Lord Jesus Christ] became poor, so that by His poverty you might become rich. (2 Corinthians 8:9)

Unclench my hands, Jesus, that I might know the joy of sharing.

Remembering the Best

Sometimes we forget the most important people in our lives: friends, spouses, parents, children. They're always there, sometimes giving, sometimes not. They tend to be like road signs that we pass so many times, we don't really need to stop, to look, or listen. Or do we?

A prayer is a conscious moment lifted up to God. We need to be conscious of loved ones, too. Recall a time they didn't make a big deal out of something we said we'd do, but didn't. Recollect a hard time you went through together and a kindness done. Relive your last hug, tears, and laughter.

Remember being right. Remember being wrong. Remember that it is the power of love that graces you with the power to belong. Turn these moments into prayers for this special person, a way of renewing your love, gratitude and devotion.

God is love, and those who abide in love abide in God, and God abides in them. (I John 4:16)

May I recall the bounty of your grace that gave me those I love, Lord.

L-I-S-T-E-N to This

Being a good friend and a good listener often go hand in hand. Here are some ways to refine your listening skills:

- Make time: life is hectic but if you are always on the go, you'll not hear much of what's being said to you.
- Show interest: If you are bored or can't listen at the moment, it's thoughtful to suggest a better time.
- Pay attention: It is easy to become distracted, but hearing only part of what's being said is to risk miscommunication and its consequences.
- Listen for feelings: body and eye language and the tone of voice can convey almost as much as the actual words.
- Ask questions: if you don't understand what's being said, ask for clarification.
- Let the speaker finish: allow the speaker – even if well-known to you – to put it in his or her own words.
- Keep confidences: once people realize that what is told to you in private remains private, your value as a listener will go way up.

The good listener makes a rare friend.

Listen to Me, says the Lord. (Jeremiah 17:24)

Redeemer, give me the courage to confide in You.

Mining the Riches of Scripture

At the bottom of this page you will find a short selection from Scripture. Hopefully you will read it and think about it for a minute or two.

But if that is the extent of your daily reading of Scripture, you are cheating yourself. Woodrow Wilson, president of the U. S. during World War I, read the Scriptures daily. He once wrote: "I am sorry for those who do not read the Bible every day; I wonder why they deprive themselves of the strength and the pleasure.

"It is one of the most singular books in the world, for every time you open it, some old text . . . suddenly beams with a new meaning.

"There is no other book that I know of . . . that yields its meaning so personally, that seems to fit itself so intimately to the very spirit that is seeking its guidance."

Resolve today to begin reading the Scriptures each day. You will be surprised at the spiritual treasures that you will receive.

Scripture is inspired by God and is useful for teaching, for reproof, for correction, and for training in righteousness. (2 Timothy 3:16)

May I find You, Lover of my soul, in every word of Scripture.

Discouraging All Kinds of Thieves

So many firs and pines have been stolen for Christmas trees recently that some homeowners came up with a new way to discourage thieves.

They sprayed the conifers in their yards with a harmless colored mixture to make them look unattractive. In a few weeks, the color sloughed off, leaving trees their natural green.

There are also times when we have to discourage people from another type of theft: stealing the good name of others.

When someone repeats malicious gossip to you, just don't reply. Change the subject. If the gossip persists, say you do not want to talk about the person.

By not listening, you protect the victim of the gossip. You also help the person gossiping who might, in time, feel shame and guilt for making spiteful comments. Make the decision to do the honorable and honest thing.

If any think they are religious, and do not bridle their tongues but deceive their hearts, their religion is worthless. (James 1:26)

From gossips and slanderers, and from being a gossip and slanderer, God deliver me.

Every Creature Prays

People of faith pray either together or alone; in words or silently. Even those who doubt God's existence may pray when they are struck by the beauty of nature, for example. "I cannot pray!" or "Why me?" can also be prayers from the heart.

And according to the Roman Tertullian, an early Christian writer, "Every creature prays. Cattle and wild beasts pray . . . As they come from their barns and caves they look up to heaven and call out . . . in their own fashion. The birds . . . lift themselves up to heaven: they open out their wings . . . and give voice to what seems to be a prayer."

Tertullian concludes by saying, "What more need be said on the duty of prayer?"

What more indeed? Join all God's creatures in worship and adoration.

You whales and all that swim in the waters . . . all birds of the air . . . all wild animals and cattle, sing praise to Him and highly exalt Him forever. (Daniel 3:57–59)

Maker, teach me to join in Creation's hymn of praise.

On Keeping Christmas

Here are ten suggestions for a happy Christmas celebration.

- Keep Jesus in Christmas.
- Consider the immensity of God's gift of His Son to humankind.
- Give Jesus the place of honor in your heart.
- Be generous toward the needy.
- Plan for the happiness of those outside your family and friends.
- Unhurriedly, calmly, enjoy Christmas music and art.
- Give gifts for the simple joy of sharing.
- Be patient and understanding with those who bear heavy burdens at Christmas.
- Teach children about Mary's Firstborn Son whose coming we are celebrating.

Jesus, the Christ, is God's gift to us. Make your celebration your gift to God.

When the fullness of time had come, God sent His Son, born of a woman, born under the law, in order to redeem those who were under the law, so that we might receive adoption as children. (Galatians 4:4–5)

Thank You, Abba, for the gift of Your Son.

Crime Victims Struggle to Recover

Victims of crime often find more pain after the initial attack. Research indicates there is a silent epidemic that is more dangerous than health and law enforcement officials had initially believed.

In the aftermath of a crime, people face an assortment of traumas. For instance, the incidence of severe depression and phobias is higher in this group than in people who have not been crime victims.

The victims of crime are not an isolated population. Figures indicate that eighteen million people have suffered problems after being crime victims at some point in their lives. Most never receive the help they need.

But in an effort to regain control of their lives, victims are finally joining forces with members of the therapeutic community and each other.

Some days we need help. Some days we need to give it. Don't be reluctant to do either.

When justice is done, it is a joy to the righteous. (Proverbs 21:15)

Redeemer, let us work for peace and justice.

A Light at the Center of Celebration

Many of us have fond memories of some special ways our family celebrated the holidays.

Austrian Edel Cech tells how her family lighted its tree on Christmas Eve: After attending a Christmas pageant in the evening, her family came home and gathered in the living room. It was dark except for one lighted candle beside the figure of the Christ Child. This was a symbol of Christ as the light of the world.

The family said the rosary, and with each prayer, Edel's father lighted a candle on the Christmas tree. When the rosary was finished, the whole room was bright, says Edel, just as it was when the angels appeared to the shepherds.

Family customs like this are beautiful not just because of the lights or the tree, but because they keep the focus on Whom Christmas celebrates, Jesus Himself.

Let us celebrate the festival, not with the old yeast . . . of malice and evil, but with the unleavened bread of sincerity and truth. (I Corinthians 5:8)

Holy Spirit, enlighten our celebrations of the feasts and fasts of our faith.

Gift-giving Etiquette

Deciding on an appropriate gift for your hostess in another country can be tricky.

In Europe, flowers are usually safe, except for roses which can show romantic interest and chrysanthemums which are used for funerals.

Be sure you give an odd number of flowers in Austria. An even number brings bad luck. In Poland, bring flowers unwrapped. In The Netherlands, gift-wrap them. In Germany, bring them wrapped and unwrap them as you present them.

In other parts of the world, flowers may not work at all. In Hong Kong or Japan, bring cookies or candy. And in Japan, wrap presents in pastels.

The formalities of gift-giving vary around the world, but the real gift is always the same: the expression of thanks and goodwill.

Store up almsgiving in your treasury, and it will rescue you from every disaster. (Sirach 29:12)

God, make me generous and gracious.

"I Felt Like a Millionaire!"

However good our intentions, all of us need a little extra motivation sometimes. Dolores Hannan of Tucson, Arizona, uses her imagination to encourage herself.

"On a teacher's salary, I have never been able to donate as much to charity as I would like," she says. "But after completing a walkathon . . . I thought of a way I could make every walk count. I save a dollar in my 'alms box' for every mile I walk. Last Christmas I was able to put a nice donation in a Salvation Army pot. I felt like a millionaire! I never miss my walk, because someone else is counting on me."

Ms. Hannan's creativity has contributed to the good health of her body and soul. And it has helped those who count on her, too. By using your imagination you can do good for others. And it can turn into good for you as well.

[Jesus] said to them, "Whoever welcomes one such child in my name welcomes Me, and whoever welcomes Me welcomes not Me but the One who sent Me." (Mark 9:37)

Lord, may healthy love of self benefit me and others.

Laugh It Up

Recent studies have found that children laugh an average of 400 times a day, while adults laugh an average of only 15 times a day.

Some doctors believe that those 385 missing chuckles and giggles could help us lead healthier lives.

Doctors have found that laughter leads to relaxation, reduction of stress, and improves muscle tone and circulation. Twenty seconds of guffawing is the aerobic equivalent of five minutes of hard rowing. Laughter also increases sensory perceptiveness and allows you to perform tasks better.

We obviously have to take laughter a lot more seriously!

When we share joyous times and moments of good humor with our loved ones, we are doing things that are good for us in more ways than one.

Rejoice with an indescribable and glorious joy. (1 Peter 1:8)

Put a smile on my lips, joy in my heart, soul and mind, Holy Spirit.

In Praise of the Messiah

When George Frederick Handel was working on the "Hallelujah Chorus" for the *Messiah,* he said, "I think I did see all Heaven before me and the Great God Himself."

A former collaborator of Handel's prepared the text for this oratorio, hoping that Handel would write the music. When Handel read the words, he was so inspired by it that he composed the whole 265-page oratorio in only twenty-four days. Handel's glorious music has, in turn, inspired listeners for more than 250 years.

After hearing the *Messiah,* the Rev. John Wesley, acclaimed Anglican preacher and founder of Methodism, wrote in his diary: "I doubt if that congregation was ever so serious at a sermon as they were during this performance."

Great music has that power to lift our hearts and draw us closer to God.

"Hallelujah! For the Lord our God the Almighty reigns. Let us rejoice and exult and give Him the glory." (Revelation 19:6–7)

May musicians give You praise, King of Kings and Lord of Lords.

An Ancient Blessing

A Bedouin shepherd discovered the 2,000-year-old manuscripts of the Essenes, a group of Jewish ascetics, in caves near the Dead Sea. The year was 1947.

Among these Dead Sea Scrolls, as we now know them, is an expansion of the so-called Levitical or priestly blessing from the sixth chapter of the book of Numbers.

It reads, "May the Eternal [God] bless you with every good and keep you from all harm. And enlighten your heart with discretion in life. And be gracious unto you with everlasting knowledge. And lift up a kindly countenance towards you for eternal peace."

Could there be any better way to celebrate a special day for a friend or family member than by praying this blessing for them?

Goodness, discretion, knowledge, eternal peace *are* the best gifts we could want for those we love.

The Lord bless you and keep you; the Lord make His face to shine upon you, and be gracious to you; the Lord lift up His countenance upon you, and give you peace. (Numbers 6:24–26)

Bless us, Lord our God, with Your strong Presence.

Friendly Persistence

A plump tabby named Jessica, adopted by a business in New Rochelle, New York, helped the receptionist greet visitors.

One day, a man and woman came in and Jessica sauntered over to welcome them. Either they were not cat fanciers or they didn't want cat hair on their dark clothing, for they ignored her.

Jessica sat down by the woman, politely tapping her skirt, just in case she hadn't noticed her. She waited, then again tapped gently. When there was still no response, she took matters into her own paws. Jessica climbed onto the woman's lap and settled down, purring loudly. By the time the receptionist came to remove Jessica, the woman had succumbed and was petting her.

After a while, Jessica went over to the man, who had put a briefcase and newspaper on his lap in self-defense. Jessica jumped onto the table beside him and sat, leaning against his arm. Laughing, the man gave in and stroked her.

The cat's friendliness in the face of indifference or hostility usually thawed the iciest of visitors. Friendliness has a way of creating warmth where there is coldness.

This is His commandment, that we should . . . love one another, just as He has commanded us. (I John 3:23)

O that my genuine love might melt the iciest heart, Loving Lord

Keeping Christmas Always

Henry van Dyke, who wrote the classic, *The Other Wise Man,* and many other stories for Christmas, believed that the holiday spirit could live every day of the year.

Here is what he had to say: "Are you willing to believe that love is the strongest thing in the world – stronger than hate, stronger than evil, stronger than death – and that the blessed life which began in Bethlehem . . . (all those) years ago is the image and brightness of Eternal Love?

"Then you can keep Christmas, and if you keep it for a day, why not always?"

Henry van Dyke was right. Why not keep the light of love and hope that is the heart of Christmas burning from one end of the year to the other?

If you do, you'll have cause to celebrate the joy of each new day, each new opportunity God gives you.

By the tender mercy of our God, the dawn from on high will break upon us . . . to guide our feet into the way of peace. (Luke 1:78–79)

O Infant God in the oxen's stall, my God, my all!

Praying and Questioning

These thoughts on prayer come from a group of rabbis and theological scholars: "Yes, there are risks in prayer. You can feel foolish, or hypocritical, or — worse — empty. This is a conversation in which there is no certainty of response.

"But at the very least you put yourself in touch with who you are and what you could be.

"You are asking the oldest, best questions in the world: 'Are You there?' 'Do You care about me?' 'What do You expect of me?'"

Prayer is indeed a way of touching your possibilities, and realizing how much God cares. Pray. Explore prayer's terrain — God's and your own.

Touch the ground of your being as you rest in God's holy presence.

Pray constantly. (1 Thessalonians 5:17)

Holy Spirit, show me how to literally "pray constantly."

One Special Festival of Light

A cinder block shattered the bedroom window of five-year-old Isaac Schnitzer. The target: a menorah, the eight-branched candelabra for Hanukkah, the Jewish festival of light.

It was the work of members of a neo-Nazi group.

Then the Schnitzers' neighbors in Billings, Montana, did something: A grassroots campaign began to distribute and display pictures of menorahs. Despite more attacks, churches, schools and thousands of individuals pitched in.

On the last night of Hanukkah, the Schnitzer family drove around their town. They saw menorahs in houses and stores and on billboards. Amazed, Isaac said, "I didn't know so many people were Jewish."

"They're not all Jewish," his mother told him. "But they're our friends." The attacks stopped.

Sometimes being a good neighbor means more than lending a lawn mower or a cup of sugar. Sometimes it demands courage.

On the twenty-fifth day of the ninth month . . . in the one hundred forty-eighth year they . . . offered sacrifice, as the law directs, on the new altar of burnt offering that they had built. At the very season and on the very day that the Gentiles had profaned it, it was dedicated. (I Maccabees 4:52–54)

Jesus, forgive me when I forget to be full of respect for other religious beliefs and other denominations.

Making Work Sacred

"Do all your work as though you had a thousand years to live, and as you would if you knew you must die tomorrow." This advice was given by the founder of the Shakers, Mother Ann Lee.

The religious group called Shakers regarded all work as consecrated to God. No task was too small to do well. The Shakers' standard of excellence soon created a market for everything they made — from pickles to chairs.

Because of its fine workmanship and graceful design, furniture made by early Shakers sells at auction today for very high prices, as much as $80,000 for a chair.

Many people think of their job and daily chores as something apart from worship. But not the Shaker who said, "A man can show his religion as much in measuring onions as in singing Glory Hallelujah."

Cooking a meal, typing a letter, repairing a car, teaching a class — whatever is done conscientiously and in a spirit of service and goodwill toward others is also a service to God. We can follow the Shaker example by doing our work to the best of our ability and making of it an offering to God.

The people did the work faithfully.
(2 Chronicles 34:12)

Redeemer, help me to understand that work done to the best of my ability is an offering, a prayer.

A Merry Christmas Greeting

E. B. White was an essayist known for his style, wit and whimsy. Here's a holiday message as charming now as when he wrote it decades ago:

"We send forth our tinseled greetings as of old, to friends, to readers, to strangers of many conditions in many places . . .

"Merry Christmas to old men asleep in libraries . . . and young lovers who got nothing in the mail. Merry Christmas to people who plant trees in city streets. . . . We send, most particularly and most hopefully, our greetings and our prayers to soldier and guardians on land and sea and in the air — young people doing the hardest things at the hardest time of life . . .

"And last, we greet all skaters on small natural ponds at the edge of woods toward the end of afternoon . . . Merry Christmas to all and to all a good morrow!"

I am bringing you good news of great joy . . . to you is born this day in the city of David a Savior, who is the Messiah . . . you will find a child wrapped in bands of cloth and lying in a manger.
(Luke 2:10–12)

Happy Birthday, Jesus, Messiah!

Celebrating a Holy Day and Holiday

Ignatius, bishop of Antioch wrote a letter to the people at Ephesus around 107 A.D. It contains a few exquisite lines on the mystery of Christmas.

> Very flesh, yet Spirit too,
> Uncreated, and yet born
> God-and-Man in One agreed,
> Very Life-in-Death indeed
> Fruit of God and Mary's seed,
> At once impassible and torn
> By pain and suffering here below,
> Jesus Christ, whom as our Lord we know.

Christmas. It's why we give presents. Have festive meals. Get together with friends and family and those long absent.

We are celebrating a birthday – Jesus'. Merry Christmas!

A Child has been born for us, a Son given to us . . . and He is named Wonderful Counselor, Mighty God, Everlasting Father, Prince of Peace. (Isaiah 9:6)

Thank You, Jesus, for coming to share our life with us.

Unique Lives, Unique Prayers

Writer John Fischer reflected on one of his worst habits: when his children tell him about something new that they have learned, he usually downplays it, saying that he learned it long ago.

His wife, however, gets excited when she hears something "new." Her jaw drops and her eyes widen, as if in amazement. Fischer used to think his wife was acting and eventually the youngsters would find out. Then he realized that she truly was experiencing something new through the discoveries her children made.

"It's the same with God," Fischer writes. "As all-knowing and sovereign as He is, I'm sure He's still eager to hear our prayers because He has never heard it quite the way we say it. We are all unique. . . . Our lives, our experiences, and our faith expressed to Him are never old."

It only takes three minutes a day to start to pray to God. He waits to hear what you have to say.

Your Maker is your husband, the Lord of hosts is His name. (Isaiah 54:5)

Let me hear Your whisper deep in my being, Loving Lord and Spouse.

Getting Untangled

It's easy to get caught up in everyday affairs. But think about this ancient monastic wisdom: The Elder said to the person of business, "As the fish perishes on dry land, so you perish when you get entangled in the world. The fish must return to the water, and you must return to the spirit . . ."

"Are you saying that I must give up my business and go into a monastery?" asked the business person. And the Elder said, "Definitely not. I am telling you to hold onto your business and go into your heart."

To balance spiritual and other needs daily, look to the example of Jesus who, Luke tells us, often rose early to pray. He was also in the habit of weekly communal worship. Make Jesus' example your challenge. Pray for wholeness and balance in the midst of daily life.

Remember your Creator . . . before the days of trouble come, and the years . . . when you will say, "I have no pleasure in them." (Ecclesiastes 12:1)

Jesus, how can we abide with each other today?

Not Just a Trifle

There's a saying that "Genius is an infinite capacity for taking pains." Whether geniuses or not, most of us have difficulty in maintaining our patience and attention to detail over time.

Still, many writers and artists would agree that talent and creativity mean little without a "capacity for taking pains."

The highly imaginative poet and painter William Blake was also a master engraver. He believed that art "cannot exist except in minutely organized particulars." And the great Michelangelo relied not just on creative energy but also on careful work. He said — and showed — that "Trifles make perfection."

Day-by-day attention to the small facets of our work, our relationships, our lives may seem like just too much trouble. But, in fact, it's the little thing that matter.

The patience of the godly will not be frustrated. (Sirach 16:13)

Creator, ever patient with us, enable us to be patient with ourselves and others.

College Students Volunteer

What are you doing today to make tomorrow better?

Some college students who are troubled by the plight of the poor and homeless are doing something about it.

A program called "Into the Streets" is one volunteer effort that puts students where their help is needed most. They work directly with adults and children affected by AIDS, homelessness, prejudice, illiteracy, and substance abuse.

The hands-on approach of "Into the Streets" helps students to better understand other people's situations. A University of Cincinnati junior said, "I worry sometimes about having enough money for school – but there are people out there who don't even have money for the bus."

These charitable young men and women are making a difference for tomorrow's world, today. There are many other ways. Choose yours.

Love does no wrong to a neighbor. (Romans 13:10)

May we respect and help each other, God.

Between Dark and Light

An ancient parable goes like this: A rabbi once asked his students how they could tell when the night had ended and the day was dawning.

One student asked: "Could it be when you can see an animal in the distance and tell whether it is a sheep or a dog?"

"No," the rabbi answered.

Another said: "Could it be when you can look at a tree in the distance and tell whether it is a fig tree or a peach tree?" Again the rabbi shook his head no.

"Well, then, when?" demanded the students.

The rabbi told them, "It is when you look on the face of any man and see that he is your brother. Because if you cannot do this, then no matter what time it is, it is still night."

Each of us can be a light in the darkness, bringing the warmth and peace of God's love to our brothers and sisters. We only need the eyes to see that we are the light of the world.

Let your light shine before others, so that they may see your good works, and give glory to your Father in heaven. (Matthew 5:16)

Holy Spirit, set me ablaze with Your grace.

In Christ's Hands

Here's a traditional Irish prayer which expresses perfectly our year-end wishes for you, our readers:

Christ's is the seed / And Christ's the harvest
Into God's garnering / May we be drawn.
Christ's is the sea / And Christ's the fish
Into God's nets / May we be turned.
From birth to age / And age to death
Your two hands, Christ, / About us be.
From death – life's end / And life's rebirth
In heaven's grace / Eternally.

May the Lord not only keep His hands around us to protect us, but may we keep our hands open to share with others His blessings and loving compassion.

You who live in the shelter of the Most High, who abide in the shadow of the Almighty, will say to the Lord, "My refuge and my fortress; my God, in whom I trust." (Psalm 91:1–2)

As one year ends, God my refuge and fortress, help me to trust in Your care during the coming year.

Movable Feasts and Holidays

Martin Luther King, Jr. Day
Presidents Day
Ash Wednesday
First Sunday of Lent
Second Sunday of Lent
Third Sunday of Lent
Fourth Sunday of Lent
Fifth Sunday of Lent
Passion / Palm Sunday
Holy Thursday
Good Friday
Holy Saturday
Easter Sunday
Mother's Day
Ascension Thursday
Memorial Day
Pentecost Sunday
Father's Day
Labor Day
Columbus Day
Thanksgiving
First Sunday of Advent
Second Sunday of Advent
Third Sunday of Advent
Fourth Sunday of Advent

How to Honor Dr. King

On the third Monday of January, we celebrate the birth of the Rev. Dr. Martin Luther King, Jr., the civil rights leader who was slain in Memphis on April 4, 1968.

Before his own death in 1984, his father, the Rev. Martin Luther King, Sr., spoke about how he would like his son's birthday observed.

"I hope there won't be firecrackers like on the Fourth of July," he said. "I hope there won't be a lot of drinking like on New Year's Eve and I hope it won't turn into the worship of materialism like on Christmas.

"I hope that the schools and churches will study the life of Dr. King and study his methods of non-violence . . . think about peace, love and brotherhood, and how to create a society where those things are more important than war, hate and violence."

How you personally observe the Rev. Dr. Martin Luther King's birthday depends on you. But let it be for you part of a life of justice, peace and respect.

Blessed are they who observe justice, who do righteousness at all times! (Psalm 106:3)

Father, remind me of what needs to be done to obtain justice for all.

On Being a Good Citizen

Thomas Jefferson once observed that "Patriotism is not a short and frenzied burst of emotion but the long and steady dedication of a lifetime."

Citizen involvement is integral to our democracy. The good citizen:

- Studies the issues, attends meetings, makes his or her views known, votes.
- Runs for office if qualified and able to do so.
- Defends the rights of all, not just some.
- Serves as a juror when called.
- Is a good neighbor to all.
- While giving primacy to individual conscience, respects and obeys lawful authority.
- Recognizes God as the ultimate grantor of all rights.

When we fail to take our citizenship seriously, our democracy's commitment to equality under the law declines. We are responsible to each other so that, as President Lincoln said at Gettysburg, "this government of the people, by the people, and for the people may not perish from the earth."

You have multiplied the nation, you have increased its joy . . . the rod of their oppressor You have broken. (Isaiah 9:3–4)

God may I see active, responsible citizenship as my thanks for Your gift of liberty under law.

Would Peter Make the Grade Today?

Charles Scholz included a letter addressed to "Mr. Jesus Christ" in a talk he gave at a health convention in Washington, D.C.

His topic: leadership. His point: leaders ought not to rely too much on consultants and other experts.

His imaginary letter to Jesus was from "the Galilee Psychological Testing Service" and was in response to a "request" that the service test "the twelve men you were considering as associates."

While the testing hadn't been completed, the service reported, it was providing the preliminary results on "Mr. Simon Bar-Jonah."

Referring to an accompanying "profile sheet," the letter said: "Mr. Bar-Jonah's personality is characterized by a dangerous rashness, overt pride and a lack of emotional stability that would no doubt be detrimental to you and your work. We feel also that his general physical appearance would create a bad image for your proposed organization. . . . We highly recommend that you do not consider Mr. Bar-Jonah as a possible associate."

Fortunately, Jesus wasn't and isn't that fussy. So undemanding is He that He has chosen us to carry on His work. He asks only a willing heart — from Peter and from us.

Make me know Your ways, O Lord. (Psalm 25:4)

Fill up what is lacking in my abilities, Jesus.

Persistence in Prayer

Have you ever felt the need to pray, but didn't know how to go about it?

Here are two suggestions.

One, set aside some time each day. It doesn't have to be long. Three minutes at the start of the day — or just before retiring — would be fine. If you give just three minutes to reflection each day, you will be surprised at the spiritual progress you will make in a few months.

Second, start simply. Say the Our Father slowly, thinking about each phrase; or read a line of Scripture and think about what it means to you. Even a poem or a passage from a favorite book can help focus your thoughts.

God did not intend prayer to be a burden, but a time to draw closer to Him — to recognize His presence and enjoy it.

When you call upon Me and . . . pray to Me, I will hear you. When you search for Me . . . with all your heart, I will let you find Me. (Jeremiah 29:12–14)

May I set aside time each day just to be in Your presence, Loving Lord.

Learning from Creation

Gandhi said, "The greatness of a nation can be judged by the way its animals are treated."

The writer of the Book of Job wrote, "Ask now the beasts, and they will teach you; the birds of the air . . . or the earth and [they] will teach you; and the fish of the sea will declare unto you."

Black Elk, Holy Man of the Oglala Sioux, said, "All things are the works of the Great Spirit."

And Walking Buffalo, another Native American holy man, said, "The whispers of God and God's love flow through all of nature."

Do we hear Creation whisper of Creation's God — and ours?

If we do, then we will act as good stewards of the garden given us and our fellow creatures by our loving God.

By His word all things hold together. We could say more but could never say enough; let the final word be: "He is the all." . . . He is greater than all His works. (Sirach 43:26–28)

Open our ears, Creator, to hear the whisper of Your love in the works of Your hands.

Thoughtful Lesson in Life

Here are some thoughts based on a seventeenth century nun's prayer. It speaks of aging, but the sentiments could apply to most folks, most of the time.

"Lord, You know better than I know myself that I am growing older and will some day be old. Keep me from the fatal habit of thinking I must say something on every subject and on every occasion. Release me from craving to straighten out everybody's affairs. Make me thoughtful but not moody: helpful but not bossy.

"I dare not ask for improved memory, but for a growing humility and less cocksureness when my memory seems to clash with the memories of others.

"Teach me the glorious lesson that occasionally I may be mistaken . . . Amen."

That's a wise prayer for anyone in any century.

How attractive is wisdom in the aged, and understanding and counsel. (Sirach 25:5)

Father, help us grow old gracefully, wisely.

On the Trail of a Comet

Halley's Comet is named for the English astronomer who first discovered its orbit, Edmond Halley.

Halley saw the comet in 1682, and proved that it was the same comet seen over England in 1531 and 1607. He predicted it would return in 1759 – a seventy-six-year cycle – and it did.

Halley's Comet's dimensions are what you might call astronomical: diameter, 100,000 miles; tail, 50 million miles long; speed, up to 140,000 miles an hour.

If those numbers boggle the mind, so will the other stupendous wonders of God's Creation. Take more time to be in awe before the wonder and mystery of Creation.

And by the way, the next time star-gazers will enjoy Halley's Comet will be in the year 2061. Where will you be then?

Teach us to number our days that we may get a heart of wisdom. (Psalm 90:12)

Lord, help us to appreciate every day of life You give us.

"I Made You"

Some people find the existence of suffering and injustice an obstacle to religious faith. A story told by the Sufis, Muslim mystics, addresses this problem:

As a man was praying, he was distracted by the people passing by. He saw the poor, the homeless, the crippled, the sick, the victims of abuse and brutality.

As he saw all these suffering people, he began to pray more earnestly. He cried, "Great God, how can a loving Creator see such things and do nothing about them?"

Then God answered, "I did do something about them. I made you."

Each of us can be God's instrument of mercy for some person who is suffering or treated unjustly.

I [Tobit] would give my food to the hungry and my clothing to the naked; and if I saw the dead body of any of my people thrown out behind the wall of Nineveh, I would bury it. (Tobit 1:17)

Remind me, Lord, that I am the instrument of Your mercy, charity and justice in this world.

Jesus' Forgiveness Is Total

Rev. Joseph Donders in *Jesus, the Stranger* writes poetically of the apostles who had abandoned Jesus, underestimated Him, given up hope. The tomb was empty. They were frightened.

What was He going to do? . . .
I think
that they could not believe their eyes
because He came to them
and because He was friendly,
as if nothing had happened,
as if they had not betrayed Him;
He seemed to have forgotten completely
He only said:
Peace . . .
He came and forgave.

Jesus forgives everybody, everything. If we can accept Jesus' forgiveness, we have the power to forgive the deepest hurt — our own brokenness and weakness.

He removes our transgressions from us . . . For He . . . remembers that we are dust. (Psalm 103:12, 14)

Lord, help me to forgive myself as quickly and totally as You do.

In His Will

Most of us spend our lives discovering God's Will for us. Or ought to, we are told.

Yet when we think we know God's will, we too often lack the courage to live that will. When we don't know God's will for us, we storm heaven to discover it.

But a lovely prayer in the *Book of Common Prayer* hints at a deeper meaning for the phrase "God's Will." The prayer begins, "Most loving Father, whose will it is for us to give thanks for all things, to fear nothing but the loss of You, and to cast all our care on You who care for us . . ."

Now when you think about it, that prayer means that God is yearning for our company. *That* is His Will.

Keep company with God. You'll both enjoy it.

A day in Your courts is better than a thousand elsewhere. I would rather be a doorkeeper in the house of my God than live in the tents of wickedness. (Psalm 84:10)

I seek You. Let me take my rest in finding You, Beauty ever ancient, ever new.

Another Repentant Thief

"When you get to heaven, look me up."

That confident headline ran over an article by Raymond C., a jail inmate in Louisiana. The convicted bank robber wrote the piece after reading the account of the Good Thief (Luke 23:32–41). In it Jesus tells one of two thieves crucified with Him, "Today you will be with Me in paradise'.

"Just imagine that," wrote Raymond C. "There was a thief, just like me, and right now he's with Jesus!"

"At that moment," Raymond C. said of the impact the passage had on him, "I felt God like I had never felt Him before. I went to my cell, got down on my knees and cried to the Lord to save my soul.

"I didn't want to be a bad guy no more; I wanted to be a good guy. I asked God to forgive me for everything I had ever done. Now I know that if I die right now I'll be with Jesus in heaven.

"Right now I am a free man. I know these stone walls and steel bars do not exist for me any more."

That's the sort of liberty that awaits anyone who embraces Christ.

The truth will make you free. (John 8:31)

In freedom, Father, I seek Your forgiveness.

The Promise of the Egg

From earliest times, eggs have symbolized birth and resurrection.

In the second century, Christians adopted eggs as a symbol of Christ's Resurrection. Wealthy people gave eggs covered with gold leaf as presents. The less prosperous colored eggs by boiling them with flowers, leaves, bark, or insects that contained natural dyes.

Eggs have continued to be used as Easter gifts. Czar Alexander III of Russia had the world's most expensive Easter eggs made for his wife late in the nineteenth century. The goldsmith Peter Carl Faberge fashioned them of enamel, gold, and precious jewels.

Today's chocolate Easter eggs may seem trifles in comparison. But their true value lies in what they represent: spiritual rebirth and new life through Christ. As Easter approaches, let us rejoice in its great promise – the promise of Resurrected life.

Just as one man's trespass led to condemnation for all, so one man's act of righteousness leads to justification and life for all. (Romans 5:18)

May I appreciate what You did – and do – for me, Jesus.

Easter Triumph and Love

The 16th century English poet Edmund Spenser has left us a wonderful Easter prayer in his Sonnet 68. Here it is — an Easter wish for you:

> Most glorious Lord of life that on this day did make Your triumph over death and sin: and having harrowed hell did bring away captivity thence captive, us to win.
>
> This joyous day, dear Lord, with joy begin and grant that we for whom You did die being with Your dear blood clean washed from sin, may live forever in felicity.
>
> And that Your love we weighing worthily, may likewise love You for the same again: and for Your sake . . . with love may one another entertain.
>
> So let us love, dear Love, like as we ought, Love is the lesson which the Lord us taught.

Easter blessings!

Jesus of Nazareth . . . has been raised. (Mark 16:6)

Enable me, Risen Savior, to love as You loved.

Being a Mother Is a Tough Job

Being a mother today is tougher than it's ever been says Clemmie Embly Webber of Orangeburg, South Carolina. The chemistry professor was once named "national mother of the year" by American Mothers, Inc. at their annual national contest.

In discussing the difficulties involved in mothering today, Mrs. Webber said she believes "the economy is a factor" because it results in "pressure to own things."

Additionally, she said, "we have not learned to budget our time." Each day there should be "a few quiet moments for the family," but "the hustle and bustle of these days" makes those moments hard to find.

Speaking of her own mother, Mrs. Webber said, "She always stressed the value of education. She taught me that if I really wanted to do something, to do the very best I could."

Probably nothing we learn has the kind of hold on us as the things we learn from our parents. Cherish wisdom and share it with the next generation.

Wise people lay up knowledge. (Proverbs 10:14)

Thank you, Father, for all that I have learned from my parents.

Living Prayer

In Bergen County, New Jersey, a little girl of five found an original way of saying her prayers.

"Thank you, God, for the trees and the flowers and the birds. Thank you for Daddy and Mommy, and my brothers and sisters."

Then, with a broad smile, she thumped her chest: "And thank you, God, for ME!

Her parents remember that on another occasion she ended her prayer with this perfect act of thanksgiving: "And thank you, God, for GOD!"

There is in children a natural sense of prayer. Some manage to preserve it throughout their lives. Instead of using routine formulas, they are able to express themselves spontaneously, to speak from the heart. Being grateful simply and naturally before God is a beautiful form of worship. It also helps us to be better human beings.

With gratitude in your hearts sing psalms, hymns and spiritual songs to God. (Colossians 3:16)

Lord God, grant that I may always give You thanks and praise.

The Start of a Prayer-Filled Tradition

Daily sessions of the United States House of Representatives and Senate open with a prayer in keeping with a tradition begun in 1787.

Benjamin Franklin, concerned because the Constitutional Convention appeared to be stalemated, suggested that each day's deliberations begin with prayer. Franklin said: "The small progress we have made . . . is, methinks, a melancholy proof of the imperfections of the human understanding . . . I have lived, Sir, a long time; and the longer I live the more convincing proofs I see of this truth, that God governs in the affairs of men. And if a sparrow cannot fall to the ground without His notice, is it probable that an empire can rise without His aid?"

From the beginning, America has acknowledged dependence on God. William Penn observed that "Those who are not governed by God will be ruled by tyrants."

And on his way to Washington, D. C., and the presidency, Abraham Lincoln said, "Without the assistance of that Divine Being . . . I cannot succeed. With that assistance, I cannot fail."

Prayer — reliance on God — becomes second nature when we discipline ourselves to make time for it each day. You are making that attempt. Persevere in good times and bad, amid chaos and peace.

Pray without ceasing. (I Thessalonians 5:17)

Jesus, show us how to abide constantly with You in prayer.

Who Is God?

It eventually happens: your child, or someone else's child, looks up imploringly and asks, "Who made the sky, and the birds, and the trees?"

You answer, "God," and your child replies, "Who is God?"

Psychologists claim that a child's concept of God will influence whether or not he or she finds the world a friendly place and whether or not children feel good about themselves.

Children have all kinds of unusual ideas about God from, "God stays up all night so he can protect us," to "God usually wears a hat."

If we have a clear idea of what we believe about God, we can share that with a child in words he or she understands. Professionals suggest we relay a message of trust, optimism and being at home in the universe. Express love, forgiveness, patience. And that while God is loving He holds His creatures to high standards.

Children readily understand the omnipotence of God. They accept that He can be everywhere all at once, that He is love.

Perhaps it is this easy acceptance of paradox that we need to relearn from our children, our teachers.

In the beginning was the Word, and the Word was with God and the Word was God. (John 1:1)

God, show me how to speak of Your goodness, Your loving faithfulness, to Your children.

Father Really Did Know Best

Singer and actress Marie Osmond believed her father helped her learn important business lessons as she was growing up. "My father happens to be a fantastic businessman," she told the interviewer. She continued that her father "insisted that we all observe what was going on around us."

"My father never said to us, 'Trust me'," she said. "Instead, he wanted us to know exactly what he was doing and why. He wanted us to take an active part in the business side of our careers; he didn't want us just sitting around, knowing that someone was taking care of us." As a result, she is able to handle both the artistic and financial aspects of her career.

Fathers are often forgotten individuals, caricatured and, at times, maligned.

This week reflect on the positive ways your father has influenced your life. If possible, thank him personally. And if you are a father, remind yourself just how important this job really is.

Hear your father's instruction. (Proverbs 1:8)

Holy Spirit, inspire fathers to set good example for their children.

Work of Mercy, Holiness

Do you ever think of your job as part of your spiritual life? Many people probably consider their daily tasks as the way they earn their living rather than their way to holiness. In fact, work is both.

According to Dorothy Day, co-founder of the Catholic Worker movement: "All work, whether building, increasing food production, running credit unions, working in factories . . . all these things can come under the heading of works of mercy."

Each person's job offers opportunities to nourish the soul as well as to put food on the table. It means not just doing a good day's work, but looking out for the "other guy" – customer and co-worker, supervisor and subordinate. And it means accepting ourselves and others as human beings, capable of mistakes and of wonderful possibilities.

Whatever your task, put yourselves into it, as done for the Lord and not for your masters . . . Masters treat your slaves justly and fairly, for you . . . also have a Master in heaven. (Colossians 3:23; 4:1)

Holy Spirit, ever at work in the world, improve employee - employer relations.

Seeking Truth, Exploring Worlds

Thor Heyerdahl of Norway fascinated the world by sailing his raft Kon-Tiki from Peru to Polynesia in 1947. He wanted to illustrate his theories of ancient seafarers who could have visited far-flung corners of the world.

Years later the explorer returned to Peru to uncover the archeological treasures of kingdoms that existed even before the Incas. In the 1990's Thor Heyerdahl offered some thoughts on Columbus and the five hundredth anniversary of his arrival in America. The occasion should have been cause to "celebrate not only the first European who came here but also the people who stood on the shores to greet him. We should call it the Great Encounter, not the Great Discovery."

Throughout history people have dared to challenge the limits of what we know. Some of their names are familiar, most are not. But all who seek knowledge and truth, who are willing to truly encounter others, deserve respect.

I determined to take [Wisdom] to live with me, knowing that she would give me good counsel and encouragement in cares and grief. Because of her I shall have glory among the multitudes and honor in the presence of the elders . . . I shall be found keen in judgment. (Wisdom of Solomon 8:9–11)

O God, Lord of mercy, give me Wisdom.

Thanksgiving: Then and Now

The story of America's first Thanksgiving is well known: in 1621 Pilgrims and Wampanoag feasted together, as an expression of peace and gratitude.

Ten years later, another day would play a part in the history of Thanksgiving. February 22, 1631, began as a day of prayer and fasting. The crops in the Massachusetts Bay Colony had failed the previous fall. The settlers were subsisting on five grains of corn a day. Then a ship arrived from England, carrying food. The day turned into one of thanksgiving for being saved. Some New Englanders still start their holiday dinner with five corn kernels in remembrance.

In the 1800s, Sarah Josepha Hale, the editor of *Godey's Lady's Book,* worked for the establishment of a national Thanksgiving day. During the Civil War, Abraham Lincoln made Thanksgiving Day an annual celebration.

Family and friends still gather to talk, to feast, to enjoy each other's company, and to give thanks. While holidays are a chance to enjoy and reminisce, they are also a chance to serve. Neighbors who are sick, lonely or poor will have something to celebrate if we are willing to turn words of thanks into deeds of kindness.

I will give thanks to the Lord with my whole heart. (Psalm 111:1)

For the wonder of my being, of Creation, of liberty under law, of religious tolerance, God be thanked!

One of Life's Necessities

Do you make time each day to pray?

Dwight D. Eisenhower, speaking of the importance of prayer said, "It is one of the simple necessities of life, as basic to the individual as sunshine, food and water, and, of course, more so."

Or as Fyodor Dostoyevsky wrote, "Be not forgetful of prayer. Every time you pray, if your prayer is sincere, there will be new feelings and new meaning in it, which will give you fresh courage, and you will understand that prayer is an education."

Prayer gives you an opportunity to thank God, to enjoy His company and to allow yourself to be transformed in all you think, say and do. Make time today to reflect on your life and your relationship with God.

Daniel . . . continued to go to his house, which had windows in its upper room open toward Jerusalem, and to get down on his knees three times a day to pray to his God and praise Him. (Daniel 6:10)

Come, Holy Spirit, come pray in me.

Purpose of a Church

Church congregations participate in many activities. They pray, celebrate, sing, dance. They feed the hungry, house the homeless, clothe the naked, provide social services, adopt poorer worshipping communities.

They exist for a variety of reasons. The Episcopal Church of the Incarnation in Dallas decided to set down a statement of purpose. The parish exists:

- To worship God.
- To proclaim God's Good News.
- To equip men, women and children to know, love and serve God here and to be happy with Him hereafter.
- To send disciples into the world.

Everything else, it seems, flows from these. What statement of purpose would you write for your church? Your self?

Religion . . . is this: to visit orphans and widows . . . and to keep oneself unstained by the world.
(James 1:27)

May my religion express itself in good deeds done in love, Jesus.

Inviting Others to Celebrate

Californians Christine Haenen and Vladimir Huber were married in a simple ceremony and went back to work the next day. A few years later, they decided to finally celebrate with a party. In lieu of gifts, they asked their guests to give at least $20 to one of four different charities.

"What do you do with ten vases?" asked the groom. "This feels better."

As a result, the couple was able to give over $1,500 to good causes. They realized that while they had everything they needed many others had nothing. Their generosity and kindness gave some other people cause to celebrate.

Celebrations take many forms. But try to remember the less fortunate, the elderly and the lonely at holidays and other special occasions.

Rejoice during your festival. (Deuteronomy 16:14)

That we might genuinely enjoy times of rejoicing, Guest at the wedding feast of Cana.

Holding "the Hand in the Night"

Spiritual writer Thomas Merton said of his life, "It's as though I were led by the hand in a night where I see nothing, but can fully depend upon the love and providence of Him who guides me."

How did Merton arrive at this insight? How did he learn to sense "the hand in the night"? Through prayer.

You can do the same by using your own words, through the use of traditional prayers and liturgies, or by wordlessly resting in God.

Worship God, the Mystery beyond understanding. Thank God for all of His gifts. Ask for help with your needs. And remember others' needs, too. Seek, choose, rest in God's will — which you will only discover in and through prayer.

And finally, translate prayer into action. God is waiting for you and so is your neighbor.

Ask and it will be given you; search, and you will find. (Matthew 7:7)

Spirit of God, help me to pray.